THE MIDDLEAGED MAN

ON THE FLYING TRAPEZE

Books by James Thurber

Thurber & Company
Credos and Curios
Lanterns and Lances
The Years with Ross
Alarms and Diversions
The Wonderful O
Further Fables for Our Time
Thurber's Dogs
Thurber Country
The Thurber Album
The 13 Clocks
The Beast in Me and Other Animals
The White Deer
The Thurber Carnival
The Great Quillow
Men, Women and Dogs
Many Moons
My World—And Welcome to It
Fables for Our Time
The Last Flower
Let Your Mind Alone
The Middle-Aged Man on the Flying Trapeze
My Life and Hard Times
The Seal in the Bedroom
The Owl in the Attic
Is Sex Necessary? (with E. B. White)

PLAY

The Male Animal (with Elliott Nugent)

REVUE

A Thurber Carnival

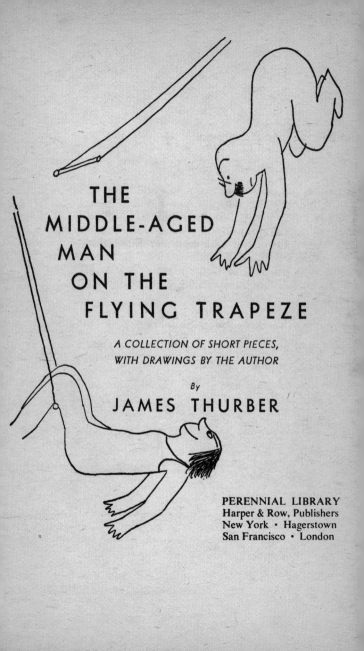

THE
MIDDLE-AGED
MAN
ON THE
FLYING TRAPEZE

A COLLECTION OF SHORT PIECES,
WITH DRAWINGS BY THE AUTHOR

By

JAMES THURBER

PERENNIAL LIBRARY
Harper & Row, Publishers
New York • Hagerstown
San Francisco • London

This book was originally published by Harper & Brothers in 1935.

THE MIDDLE-AGED MAN ON THE FLYING TRAPEZE. Copyright, 1935, by James Thurber. All rights reserved. Printed in the United States of America. No part of this book may be used or reproduced in any manner without written permission except in the case of brief quotations embodied in critical articles and reviews. For information address Harper & Row, Publishers, Inc., 10 East 53d Street, New York, N.Y. 10022. Published simultaneously in Canada by Fitzhenry & Whiteside Limited, Toronto.

First PERENNIAL LIBRARY edition published 1976

LIBRARY OF CONGRESS CATALOG CARD NUMBER: 76–41128

STANDARD BOOK NUMBER: 06–080404–1

76 77 78 79 80 5 4 3 2 1

FOR
BOB AND ELSA COATES

CONTENTS

CONTENTS

) x (

THE

MIDDLE-AGED MAN

ON THE

FLYING   TRAPEZE

I. The Gentleman Is Cold

IN THE first chill days of November it was the subject of sharp and rather nasty comment on the part of my friends and colleagues that I went about the draughty streets of town without a hat or overcoat. Once even a stranger who passed me in the street snarled, "Put on your hat and coat!" It seemed to annoy people. They began to insinuate under their breath, and even come right out and say, that I was simply trying to look strange and different in order to attract attention. This accusation was made with increasing bitterness when my hair, which I always forget to have cut, began to get very long. It was obvious, my friends said, that I walked about the city cold and miserable in the hope that people would nudge their companions and say, "There goes Jacob Thurman, the eccentric essayist."

There was, and is, no basis to these charges at all. I have reasons, and good reasons, for not wanting to, for, in fact, not being able to, wear an overcoat. I have just as good reasons about the hat, but I needn't go into them so fully. A week or so ago, however, the smirking remarks and mean innuendoes of my associates forced me one day to put on my overcoat (I couldn't find my hat and I wouldn't buy a new one, because when I try one on and peer in the triplicate mirrors they have in hat shops, I catch unexpected angles of my face which make me look like a slightly ill professor of botany who is also lost). The overcoat, which I bought in 1930, after a brief and losing battle with a sharp-tongued clerk who was taller than I am, does not fit me very well and never did fit me very well. That's one reason I don't like to wear it. Another is that it has no buttons (it didn't have any buttons after the first week) and is extremely difficult to manage in a head wind. In such a wind I used to grab for my hat with both hands, thus letting go the hold I had on my coat to keep it together in front, and the whole thing would belly out all around me. Once, in grabbing for my hat (and missing it, for I was a fraction of a second too late), I knocked my glasses off and was not only caught in a grotesque swirl of overcoat right at the corner of Fifth Avenue and Forty-fourth Street but couldn't see a thing. Several people stopped and watched the struggle without offering to help until finally, when everybody had had his laugh, a woman picked up my glasses and handed them to me. "Here's your glasses," she tittered, grinning at me as if I were a policeman's horse with a sunbonnet. I put the glasses on, gathered the coat together, and walked off with as much dignity as I could, leaving my hat swirling along the street under the wheels of traffic.

It was the twentieth of November this winter that I finally put on my overcoat for the first time. It is a heavy gray one, and looks a little like a dog bed because the strap on the inside of the collar broke and the coat had been lying on the floor of my closet for almost a year. I carried it downstairs from my hotel room to the lobby, and didn't start to put it on until I had reached the revolving doors leading to the street. I had just got one arm into a sleeve when I was suddenly grabbed from behind, a hand shot up under the coat, jerked my undercoat sharply down, and I fell backward, choking, into the arms of the hotel doorman, who had come to my assistance. He is a powerfully built man who brooks no denial of, or interference with, his little attentions and services. He didn't exactly throw me, but I took a pretty bad tossing around.

From the hotel I went, in a badly disturbed state of mind, to my barber's, and I was just reaching into a pocket of the overcoat for my cigarettes and matches when the coat was whisked off me from behind. This was done with great firmness but no skill by the colored porter and bootblack who sneaks up behind people at Joe's barbershop and tears their overcoats off their backs. This porter is not so powerfully built as the doorman at my hotel, but he is sinewy and in excellent condition. Furthermore, he was not wearing an overcoat himself, and the man who *is* wearing an overcoat is at a great disadvantage in a struggle. This porter is also a coat-tugger, belonging to that school of coat-tuggers who reach up under your overcoat after they have helped you on with it and jerk the back of your suit jacket so savagely that the collar of the jacket is pulled away from its proper set around the shoulders and makes you feel loutish and miserable. There is nothing to do about this except give the man a dime.

It wasn't, however, until I went with some fine acquaintances of mine to an excellent restaurant that night that I got into my old familiar plight with the ripped lining of the left sleeve. After dining, the gentlemen in the party were helped on with their coats by one of those slim, silent waiters with the cold and fishy eye of an art critic. He got me adroitly into the right sleeve of my overcoat, and then I stuck my left arm smoothly into the lining of the other sleeve. Running an arm into the ripped lining of an overcoat while people, both acquaintances

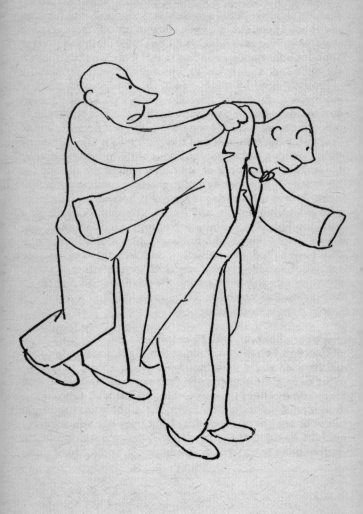

and strangers, look on and the eye of the struggling waiter gets colder and colder, is one of the most humiliating experiences known to the American male. After it was finally straightened out and I got my arm through the sleeve, I couldn't find any money for a tip; I couldn't even find a dime. I don't like to dwell on that incident.

After leaving the restaurant, we went to a theatre, and there another reason I do not like to wear an overcoat and never will wear an overcoat again reared its terrifying head. In taking off my overcoat to hand it to the unsympathetic hat-check boy, I took off with it the jacket to my dinner clothes and was left standing in the crowded and well-dressed lounge in my shirt-sleeves, with a section of my suspenders plainly visible through the armhole of my waistcoat. So speedily do hat-check boys work that my overcoat and jacket had been whisked to the back of the hat-check room and hung up under a couple of other overcoats before I could do anything about it. The eight or ten seconds that went by before I recovered my dinner jacket were among the worst moments of my life. The only worse experience I can think of was the time my suitcase flopped open on the Madison Avenue car tracks when I was hurrying to make a train at Grand Central.

I tried to pass off the episode of the dinner jacket nonchalantly, but succeeded only in lapsing into that red-faced fixed grin which no truly well-poised man-about-town ever permits himself to lapse into. I reached for my cigarettes, but I found that I had left them in a pocket of my overcoat, so in order to have something to do with my hands—for people were still staring and leering—I gracefully pulled a neatly folded handkerchief from the breast pocket of my dinner jacket, only to discover when I shook it out that it was a clean white silk sock. The last time I had dressed for dinner, I had been unable to find a fresh handkerchief, and after considerable effort had finally folded the sock and tucked it into the pocket of my jacket in such a way that it looked like a handkerchief. Of course, on that occasion I had remembered not to pull the handkerchief out. I had remembered this by grimly repeating it to myself all evening, but that had been several nights before and I had completely forgotten about the sock.

I would never have brought out all these humiliating revelations had it not been for the fact that even those persons who know me best, for a modest, unassuming man, had really come to believe that I went around town without an overcoat in order to make the same kind of impression that Oscar Wilde made with his sunflower or Sean O'Casey with his brown sweater. I simply want to be mentally at ease, and I have found out after years of experience that I cannot be mentally at ease and at the same time wear an overcoat. Going without an overcoat in bitter weather has, God knows, its special humiliations, but having a kindly old lady come up to me on the street and hand me a dime is nothing compared to the horrors I went through when I wore an overcoat, or tried to wear one.

II. The Departure of Emma Inch

EMMA INCH looked no different from any other middle-aged, thin woman you might glance at in the subway or deal with across the counter of some small store in a country town, and then forget forever. Her hair was drab and unabundant, her face made no impression on you, her voice I don't remember— it was just a voice. She came to us with a letter of recommendation from some acquaintance who knew that we were going to Martha's Vineyard for the summer and wanted a cook. We took her because there was nobody else, and she seemed all right. She had arrived at our hotel in Forty-fifth Street the day before we were going to leave and we got her a room for the night, because she lived way uptown somewhere. She said she really ought to go back and give up her room, but I told her I'd fix that.

Emma Inch had a big scuffed brown suitcase with her, and a Boston bull terrier. His name was Feely. Feely was seventeen years old and he grumbled and growled and snuffled all the time, but we needed a cook and we agreed to take Feely along with Emma Inch, if she would take care of him and keep him out of the way. It turned out to be easy to keep Feely out of the way because he would lie grousing anywhere Emma put him until she came and picked him up again. I never saw him walk. Emma had owned him, she said, since he was a pup. He was all she had in the world, she told us, with a mist in her eyes. I felt embarrassed but not touched. I didn't see how anybody could love Feely.

I didn't lose any sleep about Emma Inch and Feely the night of the day they arrived, but my wife did. She told me next morning that she had lain awake a long time thinking about the cook and her dog, because she felt kind of funny about them. She didn't know why. She just had a feeling that they were kind of funny. When we were all ready to leave—it was about three o'clock in the afternoon, for we had kept putting off the packing—I phoned Emma's room, but she didn't answer. It was getting late and we felt nervous—the Fall River boat would sail in about two hours. We couldn't understand why we hadn't heard anything from Emma and Feely. It wasn't until four o'clock that we did. There was a small rap on the door of our bedroom and I opened it and Emma and Feely were there, Feely in her arms, snuffing and snaffling, as if he had been swimming a long way.

My wife told Emma to get her bag packed, we were leaving in a little while. Emma said her bag *was* packed, except for her electric fan, and she couldn't get that in. "You won't need an electric fan at the Vineyard," my wife told her. "It's cool there, even during the day, and it's almost cold at night. Besides, there is no electricity in the cottage we are going to." Emma Inch seemed distressed. She studied my wife's face. "I'll have to think of something else then," she said. "Mebbe I could let the water run all night." We both sat down and looked at her. Feely's asthmatic noises were the only sounds in the room for

a while. "Doesn't that dog ever stop that?" I asked, irritably. "Oh, he's just talking," said Emma. "He talks all the time, but I'll keep him in my room and he won't bother you none." "Doesn't he bother you?" I asked. "He *would* bother me," said Emma, "at night, but I put the electric fan on and keep the light burning. He don't make so much noise when it's light, because he don't snore. The fan kind of keeps me from noticing him. I put a piece of cardboard, like, where the fan hits it and then I don't notice Feely so much. Mebbe I could let the water run in my room all night instead of the fan." I said "Hmmm" and got up and mixed a drink for my wife and me—we had decided not to have one till we got on the boat, but I thought we'd better have one now. My wife didn't tell Emma there would be no running water in her room at the Vineyard.

"We've been worried about you, Emma," I said. "I phoned your room but you didn't answer." "I never answer the phone," said Emma, "because I always get a shock. I wasn't there anyways. I couldn't sleep in that room. I went back to Mrs. McCoy's on Seventy-eighth Street." I lowered my glass. "You went back to Seventy-eighth Street last *night*?" I demanded. "Yes, sir," she said. "I had to tell Mrs. McCoy I was going away and wouldn't be there any more for a while—Mrs. McCoy's the landlady. Anyways, I never sleep in a hotel." She looked around the room. "They burn down," she told us.

It came out that Emma Inch had not only gone back to Seventy-eighth Street the night before but had walked all the way, carrying Feely. It had taken her an hour or two, because Feely didn't like to be carried very far at a time, so she had had to stop every block or so and put him down on the sidewalk for a while. It had taken her just as long to walk back to our hotel, too; Feely, it seems, never got up before afternoon —that's why she was so late. She was sorry. My wife and I finished our drinks, looking at each other, and at Feely.

Emma Inch didn't like the idea of riding to Pier 14 in a

taxi, but after ten minutes of cajoling and pleading she finally got in. "Make it go slow," she said. We had enough time, so I asked the driver to take it easy. Emma kept getting to her feet and I kept pulling her back onto the seat. "I never been in an automobile before," she said. "It goes awful fast." Now and then she gave a little squeal of fright. The driver turned his head and grinned. "You're O.K. wit' me, lady," he said. Feely growled at him. Emma waited until he had turned away again, and then she leaned over to my wife and whispered. "They all take cocaine," she said. Feely began to make a new sound—a kind of high, agonized yelp. "He's singing," said Emma. She gave a strange little giggle, but the expression of her face didn't change. "I wish you had put the Scotch where we could get at it," said my wife.

If Emma Inch had been afraid of the taxicab, she was terrified by the *Priscilla* of the Fall River Line. "I don't think I can go," said Emma. "I don't think I could get on a boat. I didn't know they were so big." She stood rooted to the pier, clasping Feely. She must have squeezed him too hard, for he screamed—he screamed like a woman. We all jumped. "It's his ears," said Emma. "His ears hurt." We finally got her on the boat, and once aboard, in the salon, her terror abated somewhat. Then the three parting blasts of the boat whistle rocked lower Manhattan. Emma Inch leaped to her feet and began to run, letting go of her suitcase (which she had refused to give up to a porter) but holding onto Feely. I caught her just as she reached the gangplank. The ship was on its way when I let go of her arm.

It was a long time before I could get Emma to go to her stateroom, but she went at last. It was an inside stateroom, and she didn't seem to mind it. I think she was surprised to find that it was like a room, and had a bed and a chair and a washbowl. She put Feely down on the floor. "I think you'll have to do something about the dog," I said. "I think they put them somewhere and you get them when you get off." "No, they don't," said Emma. I guess, in this case, they didn't. I don't know. I shut the door on Emma Inch and Feely, and went away. My wife was drinking straight Scotch when I got to our stateroom.

The next morning, cold and early, we got Emma and Feely off the *Priscilla* at Fall River and over to New Bedford in a taxi and onto the little boat for Martha's Vineyard. Each move was as difficult as getting a combative drunken man out of the night club in which he fancies he has been insulted. Emma sat in a chair on the Vineyard boat, as far away from sight of the water as she could get, and closed her eyes and held onto Feely. She had thrown a coat over Feely, not only to keep him warm but to prevent any of the ship's officers from taking him away from her. I went in from the deck at intervals to see how she was. She was all right, or at least all right for her, until five minutes before the boat reached the dock at Woods Hole, the only stop between New Bedford and the Vineyard. Then Feely got sick. Or at any rate Emma said he was sick. He didn't seem to me any different from what he always was—his breathing was just as abnormal and irregular. But Emma said he was sick. There were tears in her eyes. "He's a very sick dog, Mr. Thurman," she said. "I'll have to take him home." I knew by the way she said "home" what she meant. She meant Seventy-eighth Street.

The boat tied up at Woods Hole and was motionless and we could hear the racket of the deckhands on the dock loading freight. "I'll get off here," said Emma, firmly, or with more firmness, anyway, than she had shown yet. I explained to her that we would be home in half an hour, that everything would be fine then, everything would be wonderful. I said Feely would be a new dog. I told her people sent sick dogs to Martha's Vineyard to be cured. But it was no good. "I'll have to take him off here," said Emma. "I always have to take him home when he is sick." I talked to her eloquently about the loveliness of Martha's Vineyard and the nice houses and the nice people and the wonderful accommodations for dogs. But I knew it was useless. I could tell by looking at her. She was going to get off the boat at Woods Hole.

"You really can't do this," I said, grimly, shaking her arm. Feely snarled weakly. "You haven't any money and you don't know where you are. You're a long way from New York. Nobody ever got from Woods Hole to New York alone." She didn't seem to hear me. She began walking toward the stairs leading to the gangplank, crooning to Feely. "You'll have to go all the way back on boats," I said, "or else take a train, and you haven't any money. If you are going to be so stupid and leave us now, I can't give you any money." "I don't want any money, Mr. Thurman," she said. "I haven't earned any money." I walked along in irritable silence for a moment; then I gave her some money. I made her take it. We got to the gangplank. Feely snaffled and gurgled. I saw now that his eyes were a little red and moist. I know it would do no good to summon my wife—not when Feely's health was at stake. "How do you expect to get home from here?" I almost shouted at Emma Inch as she moved down the gangplank. "You're way out on the end of Massachusetts." She stopped and turned around. "We'll walk," she said. "We like to walk, Feely and me." I just stood still and watched her go.

When I went up on deck, the boat was clearing for the Vineyard. "How's everything?" asked my wife. I waved a hand in the direction of the dock. Emma Inch was standing there, her suitcase at her feet, her dog under one arm, waving goodbye to us with her free hand. I had never seen her smile before, but she was smiling now.

III. There's an Owl in My Room

I SAW Gertrude Stein on the screen of a newsreel theatre one afternoon and I heard her read that famous passage of hers about pigeons on the grass, alas (the sorrow is, as you know, Miss Stein's). After reading about the pigeons on the grass alas, Miss Stein said, "This is a simple description of a landscape I have seen many times." I don't really believe that that is true. Pigeons on the grass alas may be a simple description of Miss Stein's own consciousness, but it is not a simple description of a plot of grass on which pigeons have alighted, are alighting, or are going to alight. A truly simple description of the pigeons alighting on the grass of the Luxembourg Gardens (which, I believe, is where the pigeons alighted) would say of the pigeons alighting there only that they were pigeons alighting. Pigeons that alight anywhere are neither sad pigeons nor gay pigeons, they are simply pigeons.

It is neither just nor accurate to connect the word alas with pigeons. Pigeons are definitely not alas. They have nothing to do with alas and they have nothing to do with hooray (not even when you tie red, white, and blue ribbons on them and let them loose at band concerts); they have nothing to do with mercy me or isn't that fine, either. White rabbits, yes, and Scotch terriers, and bluejays, and even hippopotamuses, but not pigeons. I happen to have studied pigeons very closely and carefully, and I have studied the effect, or rather the lack of effect, of pigeons very carefully. A number of pigeons alight from time to time on the sill of my hotel window when I am eating breakfast and staring out the window. They never alas me, they never make me feel alas; they never make me feel anything.

Nobody and no animal and no other bird can play a scene so far down as a pigeon can. For instance, when a pigeon on my window ledge becomes aware of me sitting there in a chair in my blue polka-dot dressing-gown, worrying, he pokes his head far out from his shoulders and peers sideways at me, for all the world (Miss Stein might surmise) like a timid man peering around the corner of a building trying to ascertain whether he is being followed by some hoofed fiend or only by the echo of his own footsteps. And yet it is *not* for all the world like a timid man peering around the corner of a building trying to ascertain whether he is being followed by a hoofed fiend or only by the echo of his own footsteps, at all. And that is because there is no emotion in the pigeon and no power to arouse emotion. A pigeon looking is just a pigeon looking. When it comes to emotion, a fish, compared to a pigeon, is practically beside himself.

A pigeon peering at me doesn't make me sad or glad or apprehensive or hopeful. With a horse or a cow or a dog it would be different. It would be especially different with a dog. Some dogs peer at me as if I had just gone completely crazy or as if they had just gone completely crazy. I can go so far as to say that most dogs peer at me that way. This creates in the

consciousness of both me and the dog a feeling of alarm or downright terror and legitimately permits me to work into a description of the landscape, in which the dog and myself are figures, a note of emotion. Thus I should not have minded if Miss Stein had written: dogs on the grass, look out, dogs on the grass, look out, look out, dogs on the grass, look out Alice. That would be a simple description of dogs on the grass. But when any writer pretends that a pigeon makes him sad, or makes him anything else, I must instantly protest that this is a highly specialized fantastic impression created in an individual consciousness and that therefore it cannot fairly be presented as a simple description of what actually was to be seen.

People who do not understand pigeons—and pigeons can be understood only when you understand that there is nothing to understand about them—should not go around describing pigeons or the effect of pigeons. Pigeons come closer to a zero of impingement than any other birds. Hens embarrass me the way my old Aunt Hattie used to when I was twelve and she still insisted I wasn't big enough to bathe myself; owls disturb me; if I am with an eagle I always pretend that I am not with an eagle; and so on down to swallows at twilight who scare the hell out of me. But pigeons have absolutely no effect on me. They have absolutely no effect on anybody. They couldn't even startle a child. That is why they are selected from among all birds to be let loose, with colored ribbons attached to them, at band concerts, library dedications, and christenings of new dirigibles. If any body let loose a lot of owls on such an occasion there would be rioting and catcalls and whistling and fainting spells and throwing of chairs and the Lord only knows what else.

From where I am sitting now I can look out the window and see a pigeon being a pigeon on the roof of the Harvard Club. No other thing can be less what it is not than a pigeon can, and Miss Stein, of all people, should understand that simple fact. Behind the pigeon I am looking at, a blank wall of tired gray bricks is stolidly trying to sleep off oblivion; underneath the pigeon the cloistered windows of the Harvard Club are staring in horrified bewilderment at something they have seen across the street. The pigeon is just there on the roof being a pigeon, having been, and being, a pigeon and, what is more, always going to be, too. Nothing could be simpler than that. If you read that sentence aloud you will instantly see what I mean. It is a simple description of a pigeon on a roof. It is only with an effort that I am conscious of the pigeon, but I am acutely aware of a great sulky red iron pipe that is creeping up the side of the building intent on sneaking up on a slightly tipsy chimney which is shouting its head off.

There is nothing a pigeon can do or be that would make me feel sorry for it or for myself or for the people in the world, just as there is nothing I could do or be that would make a pigeon feel sorry for itself. Even if I plucked his feathers out it would not make him feel sorry for himself and it would not make me feel sorry for myself or for him. But try plucking the quills out of a porcupine or even plucking the fur out of a jackrabbit. There is nothing a pigeon could be, or can be, rather, which could get into my consciousness like a fumbling hand in a bureau drawer and disarrange my mind or pull anything out of it. I bar nothing at all. You could dress up a pigeon in a tiny suit of evening clothes and put a tiny silk hat on his head and a tiny gold-headed cane under his wing and send him walking into my room at night. It would make no impression on me. I would not shout, "Good god amighty, the birds are in charge!" But you could send an owl into my room, dressed only in the feathers it was born with, and no monkey business, and I would pull the covers over my head and scream.

No other thing in the world falls so far short of being able to do what it cannot do as a pigeon does. Of being *unable* to do what it *can* do, too, as far as that goes.

IV. The Topaz Cufflinks
Mystery

WHEN the motorcycle cop came roaring up, unexpectedly, out of Never-Never Land (the way motorcycle cops do), the man was on his hands and knees in the long grass beside the road, barking like a dog. The woman was driving slowly along in a car that stopped about eighty feet away; its headlights shone on the man: middle-aged, bewildered, sedentary. He got to his feet.

"What's goin' on here?" asked the cop. The woman giggled. "Cock-eyed," thought the cop. He did not glance at her.

"I guess it's gone," said the man. "I—ah—could not find it."

"What was it?"

"What I lost?" The man squinted, unhappily. "Some—some cufflinks; topazes set in gold." He hesitated: the cop didn't seem to believe him. "They were the color of a fine Moselle," said the man. He put on a pair of spectacles which he had been holding in his hand. The woman giggled.

"Hunt things better with ya glasses off?" asked the cop. He pulled his motorcycle to the side of the road to let a car pass.

"Better pull over off the concrete, lady," he said. She drove the car off the roadway.

"I'm nearsighted," said the man. "I can hunt things at a distance with my glasses on, but I do better with them off if I am close to something." The cop kicked his heavy boots through the grass where the man had been crouching.

"He was barking," ventured the lady in the car, "so that I could see where he was." The cop pulled his machine up on its standard; he and the man walked over to the automobile.

"What I don't get," said the officer, "is how you lose ya cufflinks a hunderd feet in front of where ya car is; a person usually stops his car *past* the place he loses somethin', not a hunderd feet before he gits *to* the place."

The lady laughed again; her husband got slowly into the car, as if he were afraid the officer would stop him any moment. The officer studied them.

"Been to a party?" he asked. It was after midnight.

"We're not drunk, if that's what you mean," said the woman, smiling. The cop tapped his fingers on the door of the car.

"You people didn't lose no topazes," he said.

"Is it against the law for a man to be down on all fours beside a road, barking in a perfectly civil manner?" demanded the lady.

"No, ma'am," said the cop. He made no move to get on his motorcycle, however, and go on about his business. There was just the quiet chugging of the cycle engine and the auto engine, for a time.

"I'll tell you how it was, Officer," said the man, in a crisp, new tone. "We were settling a bet. O. K.?"

"O. K.," said the cop. "Who win?" There was another pulsing silence.

"The lady bet," said her husband, with dignity, as though he were explaining some important phase of industry to a

newly hired clerk, "the lady bet that my eyes would shine like a cat's do at night, if she came upon me suddenly close to the ground alongside the road. We had passed a cat, whose eyes gleamed. We had passed several persons, whose eyes did *not* gleam ——"

"Simply because they were above the light and not under it," said the lady. "A man's eyes would gleam like a cat's if people were ordinarily caught by headlights at the same angle as cats are." The cop walked over to where he had left his motorcycle, picked it up, kicked the standard out, and wheeled it back.

"A cat's eyes," he said, "are different than yours and mine. Dogs, cats, skunks, it's all the same. They can see in a dark room."

"Not in a *totally* dark room," said the lady.

"Yes, they can," said the cop.

"No, they can't; not if there is no light at all in the room, not if it's absolutely *black*," said the lady. "The question came up the other night; there was a professor there and he said there must be at least a ray of light, no matter how faint."

"That may be," said the cop, after a solemn pause, pulling at his gloves. "But people's eyes don't shine—I go along these roads every night an' pass hunderds of cats and hunderds of people."

"The people are never close to the ground," said the lady.

"*I* was close to the ground," said her husband.

"Look at it this way," said the cop. "I've seen wildcats in *trees* at night and *their* eyes shine."

"There you are!" said the lady's husband. "That proves it."

"I don't see how," said the lady. There was another silence.

"Because a wildcat in a tree's eyes are higher than the level of a man's," said her husband. The cop may possibly have followed this, the lady obviously did not; neither one said anything. The cop got on his machine, raced his engine, seemed to be thinking about something, and throttled down. He turned to the man.

"Took ya glasses off so the headlights wouldn't make ya glasses shine, huh?" he asked.

"That's right," said the man. The cop waved his hand, triumphantly, and roared away. "Smart guy," said the man to his wife, irritably.

"I still don't see where the wildcat proves anything," said his wife. He drove off slowly.

"Look," he said. "You claim that the whole thing depends on how *low* a *cat's* eyes are; I ——"

"I didn't say that; I said it all depends on how *high* a *man's* eyes . . ."

V. Casuals of the Keys

IF YOU know the more remote little islands off the Florida coast, you may have met—although I greatly doubt it—Captain Darke. Darrell Darke. His haunted key is, for this reason and that, the most inaccessible of them all. I came upon it quite by chance and doubt that I could find it again. I saw him first that moment when my shining little launch, so impudently summer-resortish, pushed its nose against the lonely pier on which he stood. Tall, dark, melancholy, his white shirt open at the throat, he reminded me instantly of that other solitary wanderer among forgotten islands, the doomed Lord Jim.

I stepped off the boat and he came toward me with a lean brown hand out-thrust. "I'm Darke," he said, simply, "Darrell Darke." I shook hands with him. He seemed pleased to encounter someone from the outside world. I found out later that no white man had set foot on his remote little key for several years.

He took me to a little thatched hut and waved me to a

bamboo chair. It was a pleasant place, with a bed of dried palm leaves, a few withered books, some fishing equipment, and a bright rifle. Darke produced from somewhere a bottle with a greenish heavy liquid in it, and two glasses. "Opono," he said, apologetically. "Made from the sap of the opono tree. Horrible stuff, but kicky." I asked him if he would care for a touch of Bacardi, of which I had a quart on the launch, and he said he would. I went down and got it. . . .

"A newspaperman, eh?" said Darke, with interest, as I filled up the glasses for the third time. "You must meet a lot of interesting people." I really felt that I had met a lot of interesting people and, under slight coaxing, began to tell about them: Gene Tunney, Eddie Rickenbacker, the Grand Duchess Marie, William Gibbs McAdoo. Darke listened to my stories with quick attention, thirsty as he was for news of the colorful civilization which, he told me, he had put behind him twenty years before.

"You must," I said at last, to be polite, "have met some interesting people yourself."

"No," he said. "All of a stripe, until you came along. Last chap that put in here, for example, was a little fellow name of Mark Menafee who turned up one day some three years ago in an outboard motor. He was only a trainer of fugitives from justice." Darke reached for the glass I had filled again.

"I never heard of anyone being that," I said. "What did he do?"

"He coached fugitives from justice," said Darke. "Seems Menafee could spot one instantly. Take the case of Burt Fredericks he told me about. Fredericks was a bank defaulter from Connecticut. Menafee spotted him on a Havana boat—knew him from his pictures in the papers. 'Hello, Burt,' says Menafee, casually. Fredericks whirled around. Then he caught himself and stared blankly at Menafee. 'My name is Charles Brandon,'

) 25 (

he says. Menafee won his confidence and for a fee and his expenses engaged to coach Fredericks not to be caught off his guard and answer to the name of Burt. He'd shadow Fredericks from city to city, contriving to come upon him unexpectedly in dining-rooms, men's lounges, bars, and crowded hotel lobbies. 'Why Burt!' Menafee would say, gaily, or 'It's old Fredericks!' like someone meeting an old friend after years. Fredericks got so he never let on—unless he was addressed as Charlie or Brandon. Far as I know he was never caught. Menafee made enough to keep going, coaching fugitives, but it was a dullish kind of job." Darke fell silent. I sat watching him.

"Did you ever meet any other uninteresting people?" I asked.

"There was Harrison Cammery," said Darke, after a moment. "He put in here one night in a storm, dressed in full evening clothes. Came from New York—I don't know how. There never was a sign of a boat or anything to show how he got here. He was always that way while he was here, dully incomprehensible. He had the most uninteresting of manias, which is monomania. He was a goldfish-holder." Darke stopped and seemed inclined to let the story end there.

"What do you mean, a goldfish-holder?" I demanded.

"Cammery had been a professional billiard-player," said Darke. "He told me that the strain of developing absolutely nerveless hands finally told on him. He had trained so that he could balance five BB shot on the back of each of his fingers indefinitely. One night, at a party where the host had a bowl of goldfish, the guests got to trying to catch them with one grab of their hand. Nobody could do it until Cammery tried. He caught up one of the fish and held it lightly in his closed hand. He told me that the wettish fluttering of that fish against the palm of his hand became a thing he couldn't forget. He got to snatching up goldfish and holding them, wherever he went. At length he had to have a bowl of them beside the table when he played his billiard matches, and would hold one between innings the way tennis-players take a mouthful of water. The effect finally was to destroy his muscular precision, so he took to the islands. One day he was gone from here—I don't know how. I was glad enough. A singularly one-track and boring fellow."

"Who else has put in here?" I asked, filling them up again.

"Early in 1913," said Darke, after a pause in which he seemed to make an effort to recall what he was after, "early in 1913 an old fellow with a white beard—must have been seventy-five or eighty—walked into this hut one day. He was dripping wet. Said he swam over from the mainland and he probably did. It's fifty miles. Lots of boats can be had for the taking along the main coast, but this fellow was apparently too stupid to take one. He was as dull about everything as about that. Used to recite short stories word for word—said he wrote them himself. He was a writer like you, but he didn't seem to have met any interesting people. Talked only about himself, where he'd come from, what he'd done. I didn't pay any attention to him. I was glad when, one night, he disappeared. His name was . . ." Darke put his head back and stared at the roof of his hut, striving to remember. "Oh, yes," he said. "His name was Bierce. Ambrose Bierce."

"You say that was in 1913, early in 1913?" I asked, excitedly.

"Yes, I'm sure of it," said Darke, "because it was the same year C-18769 showed up here."

"Who was C-18769?" I asked.

"It was a carrier pigeon," said Darke. "Flew in here one night tuckered by the trip from the mainland, and flopped down on that bed with its beak open, panting hard. It was red-eyed and dishevelled. I noticed it had something sizable strapped under its belly and I saw its registration number, on a silver band fastened to its leg: C-18769. When it got rested up it hung around here for quite a while. I didn't pay much attention to it. In those days I used to get the New York papers about once a month off a supply boat that used to put in at an island ten miles from here. I'd row over. One day I saw a notice in one of the papers about this bird. Some concern or other, for a publicity stunt, had arranged to have this bird carry a thousand dollars in hundred-dollar bills from the concern's offices to the place where the bird homed, some five hundred miles away. The bird never got there. The papers had all kinds of theories: the bird had been shot and robbed, it had fallen in the water and drowned, or it had got lost."

"The last was right," I said. "It must have got lost."

"Lost, hell," said Darke. "After I read the stories I caught it up one day, suddenly, and examined the packet strapped to it. It only had four hundred and sixty-five dollars left."

I felt a little weak. Finally, in a small voice, I asked: "Did you turn it over to the authorities?"

"Certainly not," said Darrell Darke. "A man or a bird's life is his own to lead, down here. I simply figured this pigeon for a fool, and let him go. What could he do, after the money was gone? Nothing." Darke rolled and lighted a cigarette and smoked a while, silently. "That's the kind of beings you meet with down here," he said. "Stupid, dullish, lacking in common sense, fiddling along aimlessly. Menafee, Cammery, Bierce, C-18769—all the same. It gets monotonous. Tell me more about this Grand Duchess Marie. She must be a most interesting person."

VI. A Preface to Dogs

As soon as a wife presents her husband with a child, her capacity for worry becomes acuter: she hears more burglars, she smells more things burning, she begins to wonder, at the theatre or the dance, whether her husband left his service revolver in the nursery. This goes on for years and years. As the child grows older, the mother's original major fear—that the child was exchanged for some other infant at the hospital—gives way to even more magnificent doubts and suspicions: she suspects that the child is not bright, she doubts that it will be happy, she is sure that it will become mixed up with the wrong sort of people.

This insistence of parents on dedicating their lives to their children is carried on year after year in the face of all that dogs have done, and are doing, to prove how much happier the parent-child relationship can become, if managed without sentiment, worry, or dedication. Of course, the theory that dogs have a saner family life than humans is an old one, and it was in order to ascertain whether the notion is pure legend or whether it is based on observable fact that I have for four years made a careful study of the family life of dogs. My conclusions entirely support the theory that dogs have a saner family life than people.

In the first place, the husband leaves on a woodchuck-hunting expedition just as soon as he can, which is very soon, and never comes back. He doesn't write, makes no provision for the care or maintenance of his family, and is not liable to prosecution because he doesn't. The wife doesn't care where he is, never wonders if he is thinking about her, and although she may start at the slightest footstep, doesn't do so because she is hoping against hope that it is he. No lady dog has ever been known to set her friends against her husband, or put detectives on his trail.

This same lack of sentimentality is carried out in the mother dog's relationship to her young. For six weeks—but only six weeks—she looks after them religiously, feeds them (they come clothed), washes their ears, fights off cats, old women, and wasps that come nosing around, makes the bed, and rescues the puppies when they crawl under the floor boards of the barn or get lost in an old boot. She does all these things, however, without fuss, without that loud and elaborate show of solicitude and alarm which a woman displays in rendering some exaggerated service to her child.

At the end of six weeks, the mother dog ceases to lie awake at night harking for ominous sounds; the next morning she snarls at the puppies after breakfast, and routs them all out of the house. "This is forever," she informs them, succinctly. "I have my own life to live, automobiles to chase, grocery boys' shoes to snap at, rabbits to pursue. I can't be washing and feeding a lot of big six-weeks-old dogs any longer. That phase is definitely over." The family life is thus terminated, and the mother dismisses the children from her mind—frequently as many as eleven at one time—as easily as she did her husband. She is now free to devote herself to her career and to the novel and astonishing things of life.

In the case of one family of dogs that I observed, the mother, a large black dog with long ears and a keen zest for living, tempered only by an immoderate fear of toads and turtles, kicked ten puppies out of the house at the end of six weeks to the day—it was a Monday. Fortunately for my observations, the puppies had no place to go, since they hadn't made any plans, and so they just hung around the barn, now and again trying to patch things up with their mother. She refused, however, to entertain any proposition leading to a resumption of home life, pointing out firmly that she was, by inclination, a chaser of bicycles and a hearth-fire watcher, both of which activities would be insupportably cluttered up by the presence of ten helpers. The bicycle-chasing field was overcrowded, anyway, she explained, and the hearth-fire-watching field even more so. "We could chase parades together," suggested one of the dogs, but she refused to be touched, snarled, and drove him off.

It is only for a few weeks that the cast-off puppies make overtures to their mother in regard to the reëstablishment of a home. At the end of that time, by some natural miracle that I am unable clearly to understand, the puppies suddenly one day don't recognize their mother any more, and she doesn't recognize them. It is as if they had never met, and is a fine idea, giving both parties a clean break and a chance for a fresh start. Once, some months after this particular family had broken up and the pups had been sold, one of them, named Liza, was

brought back to "the old nest" for a visit. The mother dog of course didn't recognize the puppy and promptly bit her in the hip. They had to be separated, each grumbling something about you never know what kind of dogs you're going to meet. Here was no silly, affecting reunion, no sentimental tears, no bitter intimations of neglect, or forgetfulness, or desertion.

If a pup is not sold or given away, but is brought up in the same household with its mother, the two will fight bitterly, sometimes twenty or thirty times a day, for maybe a month. This is very trying to whoever owns the dogs, particularly if they are sentimentalists who grieve because mother and child don't know each other. The condition finally clears up: the two dogs grow to tolerate each other and, beyond growling a little under their breath about how it takes all kinds of dogs to make up a world, get along fairly well together when their paths cross. I know of one mother dog and her half-grown daughter who sometimes spend the whole day together hunting woodchucks, although they don't speak. Their association is not sentimental, but practical, and is based on the fact that it is safer to hunt woodchucks in pairs than alone. These two dogs start out together in the morning, without a word, and come back together in the evening, when they part, without saying good night, whether they have had any luck or not. Avoidance of farewells, which are always stuffy and sometimes painful, is another thing in which it seems to me dogs have better sense than people.

Well, one day the daughter, a dog about ten months old, seemed, by some prank of nature which again I am unable clearly to understand, for a moment or two, to recognize her mother, after all those months of oblivion. The two had just started out after a fat woodchuck who lives in the orchard. Something got wrong with the daughter's ear—a long, floppy ear. "Mother," she said, "I wish you'd look at my ear." Instantly the other dog bristled and growled. "I'm not your mother," she said, "I'm a woodchuck-hunter." The daughter grinned. "Well," she said, just to show that there were no hard feelings, "that's not my ear, it's a motorman's glove."

VII. Guessing Game

An article was found after your departure in the room which you occupied. Kindly let us know if you have missed such an article, and if so, send us a description and instructions as to what disposition you wish made of same. For lack of space, all Lost and Found articles must be disposed of within two months.

LOST AND FOUND DEPARTMENT
HOTEL LEXINGTON
Lexington Ave. & 48th St., New York
Per R. E. Daley.

Dear Mr. Daley:
THIS whole thing is going to be much more complicated than you think. I have waited almost two weeks before answering your postcard notification because I have been unable to figure out what article I left behind. I'm sorry now I didn't just forget the whole business. As a matter of fact, I did try to forget it, but it keeps bobbing up in my mind. I have got into an alphabetical rut about it; at night I lie awake naming articles to myself: bathrobe, bay rum, book, bicycle, belt, baby, etc. Dr.

Prill, my analyst, has advised me to come right out and meet you on the subject.

So far, I have been able to eliminate, for certain, only two articles. I never remember to take pajamas or a hairbrush with me, so it couldn't be pajamas or a hairbrush you found. This does not get us very far. I have, however, ransacked the house and I find that a number of things are missing, but I don't remember which of them, if any, I had with me at the Lexington that night: the vest to my blue suit, my life-insurance policy, my Scotch terrier Jeannie, the jack out of the automobile tool case, the bottle-opener that is supposed to be kept in the kitchen drawer, the glass top to the percolator, a box of aspirin, a letter from my father giving my brother William's new address in Seattle, a roll of films (exposed) for a 2A Kodak, my briefcase (missing since 1927), etc. The article you have on hand might be any of these (with the exception of the briefcase). It would have been entirely possible for me, in the state of mind I was in that Friday, to have gone about all day with the automobile jack in my hand.

The thing that worries me most is the possibility that what I left in my room was something the absence of which I have not yet discovered and may never discover, unless you give me some hint. Is it animal, vegetable, or mineral? Is it as big as I am? Twice as big? Smaller than a man's hand? Does it have a screw-on top? Does it make any kind of regular ticking noise when in operation? Is it worth, new, as much as a hundred dollars? A thousand dollars? Fifty cents? It isn't a bottle of toothache drops, is it? Or a used razor blade? Because I left them behind on purpose. These questions, it seems to me, are eminently fair. I'm not asking you some others I could think of, such as: Does it go with the pants and coat of a blue suit? Can it bark? Can it lift the wheel of an automobile off the ground? Can it open a bottle? Does it relieve pain? Is it a letter from somebody? Does anybody get any money out of it when I am dead, providing I keep the payments up?

I think you should let me know whether you are willing to answer yes or no to my first set of questions, as in all games of this sort. Because if you are just going to stand there with a silly look on your face and shake your head and keep repeating "Can't guess what it i-yis, can't guess what it i-yis!", to hell with it. I don't care if it's a diamond ring.

I take it for granted, of course, that I really did leave an article in the room I occupied. If I didn't, and this thing turns out to be merely a guessing game in which the answer is Robert E. Lee's horse, or something, you'll never be able to answer your phone for a whole year without running the chance of it's being me, reserving dozens of rooms in a disguised voice and under various assumed names, reporting a fire on the twenty-third floor, notifying you that your bank balance is overdrawn, pretending, in a husky guttural, that you are the next man the gang is going to put on the spot for the shooting of Joe the Boss over in Brooklyn.

Of course, I'm a little sore about the thing the way it is. If you had been a guest at my house and had gone away leaving your watch or your keyring behind, would I send you a penny postcard asking you to guess what you had left behind? I would now, yes; but I mean before this all happened. Supposing everybody did business that way. Supposing your rich and doting uncle wired you: "I'm arriving Grand Central some time next month. Meet me." Or, worse yet, supposing that instead of issuing a summons naming a definite crime or misdemeanor, the courts sent out a postcard reading: "I know what's going to happen to you-oo!" We'd all be nervous wrecks.

The only thing I see to do right now is comply with your request for a description of the article I left in that room. It is a large and cumbersome iron object, usually kept in a kitchen

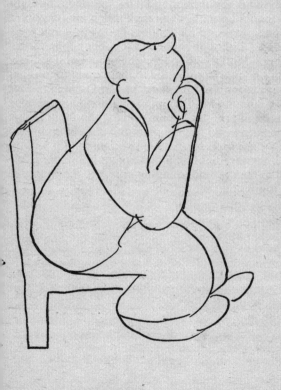

drawer, entitling my wife, upon my death, to a certain payment of money; it barks when in operation and, unless used when the coffee reaches the boiling point, will allow the liquid to spill out on the stove; it is signed by my father's name, is sensitive to light, relieves neuralgic pains, and is dark blue in color.

I have, of course, the same suspicion that you seem to have; namely, that maybe the object wasn't left behind by me but by somebody else who occupied the room before I did or who occupied it at the same time I did, without either one of us knowing the other was there. And I'll tell you why. The night that I was at your hotel, the room clerk took a message out of my box when he reached for my key. The message was for a Mr. Donovan. I looked at it and said it didn't belong to me. "You haven't a Mr. Donovan with you?" he asked. I said no, but he didn't seem to be convinced. Perhaps whatever was left behind in my room was left behind by Mr. Donovan. I have an idea that, after all, Mr. Donovan and I may have occupied the same room, since his mail was in my box; perhaps he always arrived just after I had left the room and got out each time just before I came back. It's that kind of city.

I'm glad, anyway, that I have two months before the article is returned to the insurance company or sent to the pound, or whatever. It gives me time to think.

VIII. Everything Is Wild

IN THE first place it was a cold and rainy night and the Cortrights lived eighteen miles away, in Bronxville. "Eighteen hundred miles," Mr. Brush put it, bitterly. He got the car out of the Gramercy Lane garage, snarling savagely at the garage man, an amiable and loquacious fellow who spoke with an accent and who kept talking about winter oil and summer oil, and grinning, and repeating himself. As they drove out, Mrs. Brush told her husband that he didn't have to be so mean, the man hadn't done anything to him. "He kept yelling about oil, didn't he?" demanded Mr. Brush. "I know about oil. Nobody has to tell me about oil." Mrs. Brush kept her voice abnormally low, the way she always did when he was on the verge of a tantrum. "He wasn't yelling," she said. "He'll probably ruin the car some night, the way you acted."

The drive to Bronxville was as bad as Mr. Brush expected it would be. He got lost, and couldn't find Bronxville. When he did find Bronxville, he couldn't find the Woodmere Apartments. "You'll have to ask somebody where it is," said Mrs. Brush. He didn't want to ask anybody anything, but he stopped in front of a bright little barbershop, got out, and went inside. The barber he encountered turned out to be a garrulous foreigner. Sure, he knew where eez these Woodmare Apartamen. "Down is street has a concrete breech," he said. "It go under but no up to the first raid light. Quick, like this, before turn!" The barber made swift darting angles in the air with his hand. He also turned completely around. "So not down these light, hah?" he finished up. Mr. Brush snarled at him and went outside.

"Well?" asked Mrs. Brush. She knew by his silence that he hadn't found out anything. "*I'll* go in and ask next time," she said. Mr. Brush drove on. "The guy didn't know what he was talking about," he said. "He's crazy." Finally, after many twists and turns, most of them wrong, they drove up in front of the Woodmere. "Hell of an apartment building," said Mr. Brush. Mrs. Brush didn't answer him.

The dinner, fortunately, was quite nice. Mr. Brush had expected, indeed he had predicted, that there would be a lot of awful people, but the Brushes were the only guests. The Cortrights were charming, there wasn't a radio, and nobody talked about business or baseball. Also there was, after dinner, Mr. Brush's favorite liqueur, and he was just settling comfortably into a soft chair, glass in hand, when the doorbell rang. A man and a woman were brought into the room and introduced— a Mr. and Mrs. Spreef, as Brush got it. The name turned out to be Spear. Mr. Brush didn't like them. They were quite nice, but he never liked anybody he hadn't met before.

After a flurry of trivial talk, during which Spear told a story about a fellow who had been courting a girl for fifteen years, at which everybody laughed but Brush, who grinned fixedly, the hostess wanted to know if people would like to play poker.

There were pleased murmurs, a grunt from Brush, and in a twinkling a card table was pulled out from behind something and set up. Mrs. Cortright brightly explained that one leg of the table was broken, but she thought it would hold up all right. Mr. Brush didn't actually say that he thought it wouldn't, but he looked as if he did.

Mr. Spear won the deal. "This is dealer's choice, Harry," his hostess told him. "Change on each deal." Harry squealed. "O. K." he said. "How about a little old Duck-in-the-Pond?" The ladies giggled with pleasure. "Whazzat?" grumbled Brush. He hated any silly variation of the fine old game of poker. He instantly dropped out of the hand and sat staring at Mr. Spear. Mr. Spear, it came to him, looked like Chevalier. Mr. Brush hated Chevalier.

The next deal fell to Brush and he immediately named straight poker as his game. Mrs. Spear said she was crazy about Duck-in-the-Pond and why didn't they just keep on playing that? "Straight poker," said Mr. Brush, gruffly. "Oh," said Mrs. Spear, her smile vanishing. Mr. Brush won the straight-poker hand with three of a kind.

Mrs. Spear was the next dealer. "Seven-card stud," she said, "with the twos and threes wild." The women all gave little excited screams. Mrs. Cortright said she was crazy about seven-card stud with something wild. Mrs. Spear said she was, too. Mr. Brush said yah. Mrs. Spear won the hand with four kings —that is, two kings, a deuce, and a trey. Mr. Cortright, the next dealer, announced that they would now play Poison Ivy. This was a nuisance Mr. Brush had never heard of. It proved to be a variation of poker in which each player gets four cards, and five others are placed face down on the table to be turned up one at a time. The lowest card, when all are turned up, becomes the wild card. Mr. Brush rolled his cigar from one corner of his mouth to the other, and narrowed his eyes. He scowled at Chevalier, because Chevalier kept repeating that Poison Ivy was the nuts. Brush folded up his hand and sat stiffly in his chair, rolling his cigar and grunting. Four aces won that hand, and in doing so had to beat four other aces (there were two fours in the hand on the table, and they were low).

So the game went wildly on, with much exclaiming and giggling, until it came Mr. Brush's time to deal again. He sat up very straight in his chair and glared around the table. "We'll play Soap-in-Your-Eye this time," he said, grimly. Mrs. Spear screeched. "Oh, I don't know that!" she cried. Brush rolled his cigar at her. "Out West they call it Kick-in-the-Pants," he said. Mrs. Brush suggested that they better play Duck-in-the-Pond again, or Poison Ivy. "Soap-in-Your-Eye," said Brush, without looking at her. "How does it go?" asked Cortright.

"The red queens, the fours, fives, sixes, and eights are wild," said Mr. Brush. "I'll show you." He dealt one card to each person. Then he dealt another one around, face up this time. "Ah," he exclaimed, "Mrs. Spear draws a red queen on the second round, so it becomes forfeit. It can be reinstated, however, if on the next round she gets a black four. I'll show you." Mr. Brush was adroit with cards and he contrived it so that Mrs. Spear did get a black four on the next round. "Ho," said Brush, "that makes it interesting. Having foured your queen, you can now choose a card, any card, from the deck." He held up the deck and she selected a card. "Now if you don't want that card," continued Brush, "you can say 'Back' or 'Right' or 'Left,' depending on whether you want to put it back in the deck or pass it to the person at your right or the person at your left. If you decide to keep it, you say 'Hold.' The game, by the way, is sometimes called Hold Back or Right and Left. Get it?"

"I don't think so," said Mrs. Spear. She looked vaguely at the card she had drawn. "Hold, I guess," she said.

"Good," said Brush. "Now everybody else draws a card." Everybody did, Mrs. Brush trying to catch her husband's eye, but failing. "Now," said Brush, "we each have four cards, two of which everybody has seen, and two of which they haven't. Mrs. Spreef, however, has a Hold. That is, having black-foured her red queen, she is privileged to call a jack a queen or a trey a four or any other card just one point under a wild card, a wild card. See?" Nobody, apparently, saw.

"Why don't we just play Poison Ivy again?" asked Mrs. Brush. "Or a round of straight poker?"

"I want to try this," said Brush. "I'm crazy about it." He dealt two more cards around, face down. "We all have six cards now," he went on, "but you can't look at the last two—even after the game is over. All you can look at is the four cards in your hand and this one." He put a card face down in the middle of the table. "That card is called Splinter-Under-Your-Thumb and is also wild, whatever it is," he explained. "All right, bet." Everybody was silent for several seconds, and then they all checked to him. Brush bet five chips. Mrs. Spear, encouraged in a dim way by the fact that she had black-foured her red queen, thus reinstating it after forfeit, stayed, and so did Mrs. Cortright (who always stayed), but the others dropped out. The two ladies put in five chips each, and called Mr. Brush. He turned up the card in the middle of the table—the queen of diamonds. "Hah!" said Brush. "Well, I got a royal flush in spades!" He laid down the four of diamonds, the eight of hearts, and a pair of sixes. "I don't see how you have," said Mrs. Spear, dubiously. "Sure," said Brush. "The queen of diamonds is a wild card, so I call it the ace of spades. All my other cards are wild, so I call them king, queen, jack, ten of spades." The women laid their hands down and looked at Brush. "Well, you both got royal flushes, too," he said, "but mine is spades and is high. You called me, and that gave me the right to name my suit. I win." He took in the chips.

The Brushes said good night and left shortly after that. They

went out to the elevator in silence, and in silence they went out to the car, and in silence they drove off. Mr. Brush at last began to chortle. "Darn good game, Soap-in-Your-Eye," he said. Mrs. Brush stared at him, evilly, for a full minute. "You terrible person," she said. Mr. Brush broke into loud and hearty laughter. He ho-hoed all the way down the Grand Concourse. He had had a swell time after all.

IX. The State of Bontana

I AM sure that it must have been Dudley Pierce who introduced Oral Categories into our little group. A curious light comes into his eyes when people gather together in a comfortable room and begin to talk. Dudley can hardly wait for a lull in the conversation; very often, indeed, he makes a lull in the conversation: "How about some Oral Categories?" he will shout, much to the annoyance of whoever is saying to whomever else, "What! You don't know André Simon's 'The Art of Good Living'? But one cannot ——"

Oral Categories, as you may know, goes like this. Whoever is It takes a letter, say M, and the others wait, more or less breathlessly, for him to name a category. Suppose he has taken M and says, "A make of automobile!" Then the first person who names an automobile beginning with M—Marmon, for example—wins a point. The first player to win five points is It and he, in turn, selects another letter and names more categories, and so it goes until people get tired of it, or bored, or, as has been happening more and more often in our circle, annoyed, hurt, or downright angry.

The game has, as a matter of fact, thrown a clear white light for me upon some of my friends who, until it was instituted among us, were simply the pleasant, conventional figures that most of our friends are—those friends, I mean, whom we rarely become intimate with but nevertheless think we know quite well by mingling with them, year in and year out, at parties. They have taken on color and character for me, dropped their masks, spoken in unfamiliar tones, stood out sharply in strange and new postures.

There is, for instance, Viola Drake. The fact that she was married, about a year ago, to Holman Drake brought her into our group. Until Categories came along we had all supposed that her silences draped, charmingly enough, an almost total lack of interest in anything except Holman. Certainly no one had been able to draw her out on any subject (I see now that no one tried the right ones). She became, quite suddenly, articulate and varied in this peculiar game. I recall the night that the letter A and the category Bird came up. "Avocet," said Viola in her low, cool voice before anyone else spoke (most of us shout out our answers excitedly). There was a rustle and a muttering. Then: "What kind of a bird is that?" demanded Myra Hertzman, shrilly. "I never heard of a whatever-it-is." Myra's voice always has the pitch and fever of a person describing a train wreck. None of the rest of us, I think, had heard of an avocet either. "It's a water bird with long legs and a long curved bill," said Viola. Somebody looked it up in a dictionary and there, of course, it was.

Michael Lindsey announced, in the admiring pause that followed, that we had all missed Auk. "Yes," said Kaley Geren, "and Albatross." Then somebody else observed that there didn't seem to be any other birds than those three whose names began with A. "Not many, certainly," said Viola. I asked her if she knew any more. "Well," she said, "there are the Ash-throated Flycatcher and the Arkansas Kingbird, if you would allow them. They're very real," she said to Myra, smiling. We were impressed; there was a murmur of approbation. When Viola a moment later said "Arachne" and won the next category also, I began to realize for the first time that this lady had been beaten into her silences by our continuous gabble about liquor and books and economics.

But if our little game has brought Viola into flower, so to speak, it has definitely made enemies of Michael Lindsey and Kaley Geren, who, up until Categories, had maintained a polite friendship despite their fundamental differences of opinion about Chianti, John Dos Passos, and Marxism. It began the night that Lindsey had the letter B and named as a category "a kind of camel." Nobody answered for many minutes. Lindsey smiled his superior smile. "Give up?" he asked. "Wait a second," said Geren. "I know it as well as you do." "*Big* camel!" squealed Myra Hertzman, giggling. Myra always has her joke, her series of jokes, about every letter and category that are named. "How about a camel named Bert?" she added. Geren, who was trying to think, frowned at her. "Give up?" said Lindsey, again. "No, no," said Geren. "Wait a second." Lindsey's smile became definitely smug. Geren, I feel sure, actually knew the word, but he had groped his way into a morass of B's. The psychological pitfalls and illusions of the game are many. The answer in this particular case—Bactrian, of course, though none of us could think of it—was on the end of Geren's tongue, on the edge of his mind, but so were a lot of other words beginning with B, including Big Camel and Bert Camel. In the end, bewitched by alliterations, Geren abruptly shouted out "Bucephalus!" thinking, for a wild moment, that he had got his hands on the word he was seeking for. Lindsey laughed. "Bucephalus was the war horse of Alexander the Great, Kaley," he said, patronizingly. "Of course it was," said Kaley. "I know that. I know that as well as you know it, but—" "But you just couldn't think of it, could you, dear?" asked his wife, innocently. She was, I think, merely trying to avert what she discerned as approaching trouble between the two, but Kaley took it to mean that she thought he didn't know what Bucephalus was. He understands the nuances of her inflections better than I do, but I think he was wrong. "Certainly I know it!" snapped Kaley. "Everybody knows it!" "I don't know it!" screamed Myra. "Anyway, nobody's got the answer to the big bad camel yet!" That brought Geren back to that. He had to give up, still insisting he knew but couldn't think. "Bactrian," said Lindsey smoothly. Geren sniffed and made a gesture. Lindsey lighted a cigarette. That was the beginning of a growing formality between them and, as far as I know, a widening chasm between the Gerens themselves, for I could foresee a cold, tense argument in their car on the way home: "Just exactly why you see fit to hold me up to ridicule before that fellow Lindsey is, of course, your own . . ."

Nobody (unless it is Garrison) has been made more miserable by our favorite game than John Almond. Almond has as fine a mind and as wide a general knowledge as any man I know, but he invariably becomes mind-tied when Oral Categories is started. If you took R and then said "Name a flower" he would be unable, for some strange reason, to think of Rose. He just sits there, staring at the floor, a heavy, angry look on his face. I daresay the machinery of his mentality is too complex for him to turn out instantly an obvious and meagre little word. But he is sensitive and easily annoyed. The game has got to him. He worries about it, hates it, but comes back to it the way an unlucky player comes back to the roulette table. Grace Almond, confident of his potential superiority, has taken to railing at him merrily during the games. "Poor Johnny didn't do very well at his lessons in school," she will say. That always gives Lindsey —and Myra Hertzman—a laugh (Myra would get a laugh out of any sudden announcement, even that someone had dropped dead). Almond pretends to take the joking in all good humor, but recently it has been apparent to me that he forces his smile. I think that on their way home from the last party the Almonds must have "had it out," because John did not win one point that night and Grace blithely called attention to it at the door and patted his cheek and said, "Poor Johnny didn't do so well at his lessons in school." She doesn't hit on many little quips and when she does she holds onto them. I think this one had the effect on John of a half-finished mug of ale that has stood all night and I imagine that he said so and I imagine that she slept in the guest-room, crying.

It was Garrison, however, who took the worst beating at our last party. He doesn't come to our parties often, has never enjoyed the game, and rarely gets into it, preferring to sit in a corner and read a book or (as I have often noticed) look at Louise Grayson with furtive eyes. He did get into the game this last night, however. Lillian Garrison, jumpy, small, with a rasping voice, fairly tugged him into it: "Now you're *not* going to *sit* there and *read* all evening!" He came into it the way Jeffries came into the ring with Jack Johnson, if you happen to remember.

Garrison is, or was, one of the ablest executives in town, a quiet, fiftyish, forceful man who loves the last firm dignified word and is bred to a posture of dominance. In the very first category his "Pierce-Arrow" trailed in a bad third behind his own wife's "Packard" and Lindsey's "Peerless" and he felt, I could see, a little silly, for he had barked out his futile answer in a voice of peremptory command. It was a bad start and for several categories thereafter he maintained a haughty silence. Lindsey eventually won and became It again—for the third or

fourth time—whereupon Kaley Geren got up and muttered something about he guessed he'd mix another drink.

Lindsey took the letter B. "Name a state in the Union!" he snapped. "Boston!" shouted someone, excitedly, and then flushed as the others hooted. Of course there was then a long silence, for there is no state beginning with B. "Bassachusetts!" squealed Myra Hertzman. "Bidaho! Butah! Bontana!"

"All right," said Lindsey, finally. "There is no state with B. All right, I'll take—*a kind of bird!*"

"Beagle!" roared Garrison instantly, very erect, red in the face, a bit pontifical. He had been beautifully tricked by Myra's Bidaho, Butah, etc., into putting a B in front of Eagle. Everybody, of course, shouted with laughter. It was a long time dying down. Myra Hertzman laughed till she cried. Garrison laughed, too, but in a strange, choked, artificial way, as if he were being sick in an airplane. He crossed his legs and flung one arm over the back of his chair and glared at Myra as if he would have liked to choke her slowly and pleasurably to death. He didn't look at Louise Grayson. "B-b-beagle," chortled Myra, with tears streaming. "He said Beagle!" Dudley Pierce quietly won that round, in the confusion, with Barnswallow.

"All right, all right!" said Lindsey. "Here comes another. Here comes another. Ready? *A kind of dog!*"

"Beagle," said Viola Drake instantly, in her cool, even voice. Nobody else, I am sure, would have thought of saying it: we had all been tricked again as far as naming that particular breed of dog went, all except the inimitable Viola—and Kaley Geren, who was out in the kitchen moodily mixing drinks. Garrison apparently took Viola's answer as the further rubbing in of an insult. His face became heavily flushed again. Presently he observed that it was infernally late. I imagine that on the way home he suddenly "began on" Mrs. Garrison. "*Beagle!* Bah! Bird-dog, Baffin Bay hound, Bulldog, Boxer!" He probably shouted at her, pounding the steering wheel with one gloved hand. "The hell with all those shallow-pated people! The hell with all of them, especially that simpering, giggling, empty-headed —— — – —— of a Hertzman woman!"

It is, I am sure, a bad game; a bad game for friends, unless they are the very best of friends. It is much better to play some nice, comfortable card game—say Red Dog.

X. Mr. Pendly and the
Poindexter

MR. PENDLY hadn't driven the family car for five years, since, to be exact, the night of the twenty-third of October, 1930, when he mistook a pond for a new concrete road and turned off onto it. He didn't really drive into the pond, only hovered at the marge, for Mrs. Pendly shut off the ignition and jerked the emergency brake. Mr. Pendly was only forty-two, but his eyes weren't what they had been. After that night, Mrs. Pendly always drove the car. She even drove it during the daytime, for although Mr. Pendly could see in the daytime, his nerve was gone. He was obsessed with the fear that he wouldn't see the traffic lights, or would get them mixed up with lights on storefronts, or would jam on his brakes when postmen blew their whistles. You can't drive toward a body of water thinking it's made of concrete without having your grip on yourself permanently loosened.

Mr. Pendly was not particularly unhappy about the actual fact of not driving a car any more. He had never liked to drive much. It galled him slightly that his wife could see better than he could and it gave him a feeling of inferiority to sit mildly beside her while she solved the considerable problems of city traffic. He used to dream at night of descending, in an autogiro, on some garden party she was attending: he would come down in a fine landing, leap out, shout "Hahya, Bee!," sweep her into the machine, and zoom away. He used to think of things like that while he was riding with her.

One day Mrs. Pendly said she thought they ought to trade in the old car for another one. What she had in mind was a second-hand Poindexter—she was tired of small cars. You could, she said, get perfectly marvellous bargains in 1932 and 1933 Poindexters. Mr. Pendly said he supposed you could. He didn't know anything about Poindexters, and very little about any automobile. He knew how to make them go and how to stop them, and how to back up. Mrs. Pendly was not good at backing up. When she turned her head and looked behind her, her mind and hands ceased to coördinate. It rather pleased Mr. Pendly that his wife was not good at backing up. Still, outside of that, she knew more about cars than he ever would. The thought depressed him.

Mrs. Pendly went to the Poindexter Sales Company, up near Columbus Circle, one day, spent an hour looking around the various floors with a salesman named Huss, and located finally what she described to her husband that evening as a perfectly lovely bargain. True, it was a '31 model, but a late '31 model and not an early '31 model. Mr. Pendly said he didn't think there ever were two models in one year, but she said Mr. Huss told her there were, that everybody knew there were, and that you could tell by the radiator cap.

She took Mr. Pendly up to the Poindexter place the next afternoon to see the car. They had to wait a long time for Mr. Huss. Mr. Pendly got restless. All the shining Poindexter 16's in the main showroom seemed to him as big as hook-and-ladders and as terrifying. He worried because he knew Mr. Huss would expect him to ask acute technical questions about the car, to complain of this and that. Mr. Huss, finding out that Mr. Pendly didn't know anything at all about automobiles, would sniff in surprise and disdain. A husband whose wife drove the car!

Mr. Huss turned out to be a large, vital man. Mr. Pendly was vital enough, but not as large as Mr. Huss. Their meeting was not much fun for either one. As they got into an elevator to go to the sixth floor, where the lovely bargain was, Mr. Huss kept referring to it as a nice job. The sixth floor was filled with second-hand cars and with mechanics, pounding and buffing and tinkering. Mr. Pendly had the same feeling in the presence of mechanics that, as a child, he had had during church sermons: he felt that he was at the mercy of malignant powers beyond his understanding.

When they stood in front of the Poindexter that Mrs. Pendly had picked out, Huss said to Mr. Pendly: "Whatta you think of that for a piece of merchandise?" Mr. Pendly touched a front fender with his fingers. The salesman waited for him to say something, but he didn't say anything. The only part of a car that Mr. Pendly could think of at the moment was the fan belt. He felt it would be silly to ask to see the fan belt. Maybe Poindexters didn't have fan belts. Mr. Pendly frowned, opened the back door, and shut it. He noticed the monogram of the previous owner on the door. "That monogram," said Mr. Pendly, "would have to come off." Since it seemed that this was all Mr. Pendly had to say, his wife and Mr. Huss ignored him and got into an intricate talk about grinding valves, relining brakes, putting in a new battery. Mr. Pendly felt the way he used to in school when he hadn't prepared his homework. He waited for an opening to cut in on the conversation and thought he saw one when Mrs. Pendly said that she didn't like the car not having a vacuum pump. Mr. Pendly jumped to the conclusion that a vacuum pump was something you could buy and put under the back seat, like a fire-extinguisher. "We could pick up a vacuum pump in any accessory shop," he said. Both his wife and Mr. Huss gave him a surprised look and then went on to the question of the rear tires.

Mr. Pendly wandered sadly over to where a mechanic was lying under a big car. As he got there, the mechanic crawled out from under, jumped up, and brushed against Mr. Pendly. "Look out, Bud," said the mechanic, who was chewing tobacco. Bud walked back to where his wife and Mr. Huss were. He had suddenly thought of the word "transmission," and had some idea of asking Mr. Huss about that. It occurred to him, however, that maybe free-wheeling had done away with transmission and that he would just be showing his ignorance. Mr. Huss was trying to get the luggage compartment at the back of the Poindexter open, because Mrs. Pendly said she had to see how large it was. The key wouldn't work. Mr. Huss shouted for somebody named Mac, and presently the chewing mechanic walked over. He couldn't open the compartment either, and went away. Mrs. Pendly and the salesman walked off to look at the compartment on a similar car, and Mr. Pendly set to work. In a few minutes he found out what was the matter. You had to press down on the cover and then turn the key! He had the back open when his wife and Huss returned. They didn't pay any attention to it. They were talking about mileage.

"I got the back open," said Mr. Pendly, finally.

"This was a chauffeur-driven car," said Mr. Huss. "And it was handled like a watch. There's another hundred thousand miles in it."

"The front seat would have to be lowered," said Mrs. Pendly. "I couldn't be stuck way up in the air like that."

"We'll take care of that," said Huss. "That'll be easy."

"You want to see into the back now?" asked Mr. Pendly.

"And you'd be sure to have the brakes tested?" Mrs. Pendly said to Huss.

"Those brakes will be A-1 when the job leaves this room," said Huss. "We never turn out a piece of merchandise here that isn't A-1."

Mr. Pendly shut the baggage compartment. Then he opened it again. He did this a couple more times.

"Come on, Bert," his wife said.

On the way home—Mrs. Pendly had decided to think the bargain over, although Huss said somebody else would snap it up if she didn't snap it up—Mr. Pendly sat beside his wife in their old car and thought. She prattled along about the Poindexter but he didn't really hear, although now and then he grunted some answer in a monotone. He was imagining that, as he sauntered over to Mac, Mac got out from under the big car he was working on and said: "Well, it's got me licked." Mr. Pendly smiled. "Yeah?" he said, slowly removing his coat and vest. He handed them to Mac. Then he crawled under the car, looked the works over coldly, tinkered delicately and expertly with a couple of rods and a piston, tightened a winch gasket, blew softly into a valve, and crawled out again. He put on his coat and vest. "Try her now," he said, indifferently, to Mac. Mac tried her. She worked beautifully. The big mechanic turned slowly to Mr. Pendly and held out an oily hand. "Brother," said Mac, "I hand it to you. Where did you ev——?"

"What's the matter; are you in a trance or what?" asked Mrs. Pendly, pulling her husband's sleeve. He gave her a cold, superior look.

"Never mind about me," he said.

XI. The Indian Sign

"MR. PINWITHER is doing wonders with the new Cora Allyn letter," Mrs. Bentley told her husband. He winced slightly. Three letters about the old lady hadn't been enough; somebody had had to turn up another one.

"That's fine," said Mr. Bentley, taking off his overcoat and hanging it up in the hall closet.

"It's all about their moving to New Milford—in 1667," said Mrs. Bentley. "There's nothing new in it, he says, about the Indians." She seemed disappointed.

"That's fine," said Mr. Bentley again. His wife, on the verge of a new eagerness, apparently didn't hear.

"*And,*" she said, "Cora learned a new word today!" *This* Cora, Mr. Bentley knew, was of course his little daughter. He really meant his "That's fine" this time. Still, he winced again. He had wanted to name his daughter Rosemary, after a dream. But his wife and all the stern and silly pride of the Allyns had been behind "Cora." Since a certain day almost three hundred years ago the first female born into every ramification of the Allyn family had been named Cora: "After old Cora Cora herself," as Henry Bentley said at the Comics' Club the night his daughter was born.

The original Cora Allyn, his little girl's great-great-great-great-great-grandmother, had slain nineteen Pequot Indians single-handed in an incredible and dimly authenticated struggle near New London, Connecticut, in 1643, or 1644. The Allyns could never be positive of the year, for the letters bearing upon the incident were almost three centuries old, yellow and brittle and written crisscross, the thrifty and illegible Colonial method of saving postage charges. Two were undated and the date of the other was faded and tricky, like all of the writing in the three priceless heirlooms of the Allyn family. The letters purported to have been written by one Loyal Holgate, supposedly a young divine, and—Bentley had examined them carefully, or as carefully as anyone who was not an Allyn was allowed to—there apparently *were* passages in them about one Cora Allyn's having slain nineteen Indians. Some of the most eminent antiquarians in the country, including Mr. Pinwither, had pored over the letters. They had all but one brought out of the vague, faint scrawlings virtually the same story of the early New England lady's heroic deed. The saturnine Murray Kraull had, it is true, doubted that the word "nineteen" was really "nineteen" and even that "Pequots" was "Pequots." He had, indeed, gone so far as to suggest that the phrase might be "no male peacocks," for which heresy he had practically been hustled out of Mrs. Bentley's mother's house. The other experts had all conformed, however, to the letter—and the number—of the legend. In Henry Bentley's mind, as in Mr. Kraull's, there would always remain a doubt.

Mr. Bentley, quietly and in secret, had long been elaborating on his doubt. So far as he had been able to find out, there was no record of a Cora Allyn who had slain nineteen Indians. There had been a rather famous incident in which a band of Pequots killed a Mrs. Anne Williamson, a Massachusetts woman who had settled near Stamford, but that was all. Once, to make a dinner topic, he had tossed out timidly to his wife that he had come upon an old history of the state at his office and so far had found in it no reference to any woman who had killed nineteen Indians. Mrs. Bentley's quick, indignant look had caused him to mumble the rest of his suspicions into his shirt-front. It was the closest he ever came to expressing openly his feeling in the matter.

"The new letter," said Mrs. Bentley, as they walked into the living-room, "tells some more about Rockbottom Thraillkill, the minister who established the third church in what is now New Milford. It was called Appasottowams then, or something like that. It is all in Mr. Pinwither's report."

"That's close enough," said Mr. Bentley. He strove to change the subject. "What did my little girl say today?" he asked.

"Cora? She said 'telephone.'"

"That's fine," said Mr. Bentley. It was terrible the way he allowed the name Cora to affect him. There were literally hundreds of Coras among his wife's connections. They kept recurring, like leaf blight, among the spreading branches of the Allyn family. And scarcely a day went by but what someone alluded to the first, great Cora. He encountered her glib ghost at all family gatherings, on all holidays, and before, during, and after every family ceremony, such as marriage, birth, christening, divorce, and death.

Mrs. Bentley talked about the small excitements of her day during dinner. Her husband affected to listen, and now and then gave a sympathetic grunt, but he was quietly contemplating that early American heroine who was so damnably intertwined with his life. Supposing that the story about her *were*

true? Why be so insistently conscious and so eternally proud of an ancestor who killed nineteen Indians? Her open-mouthed, wild-eyed gestures during the unmatronly ordeal, the awkwardness of her stance, the disarray of her apparel, must have been disturbingly unattractive. The vision of his little daughter's forebear, who up to her great hour had undoubtedly depended rather charmingly upon a sturdy pioneer husband, suddenly learning that she was more than a match for nineteen males affected Henry Bentley dismally; it saddened him to be continually carried back along the rocky, well-forgotten roads of American life to the prophetic figure of Cora Allyn, standing there against the sky, with her matchlock or her hunting knife or her axe handle, so outrageously and significantly triumphant.

Henry had often tried to get a picture of the famous Cora's husband, old Coppice Allyn. There was little mention of him in the frail letters of almost three centuries ago. Old Coppice was rarely mentioned by the Allyns, either; he remained staunch but indistinct, like a figure in the background of a wood-cut. He had cleared away trees, he had built a house, he had dug a well, he had had a touch of brain fever—things like that: no vivid, red, immortal gestures. What must he have thought that April evening (not "April" but "apple," Kraull had made it out) when he came home from the fields to find a new gleam in his wife's eyes and nineteen new corpses under her feet? He must have felt some vague, alarming resentment; he must have realized, however dimly, that this was the beginning of a new weave in the fabric of life in the Colonies. Poor old Coppice!

"I want to show you," said Mrs. Bentley after dinner, "Mr. Pinwither's report. Of course it's just a preliminary. Mother sent it over."

"That's fine," said Mr. Bentley. He watched his wife go out of the room and tried to be glad that she, at least, was not a

Cora; her oldest sister held that honor. That was something. Mr. Bentley seized the chance, now that he was alone, to reflect upon his latest clandestine delving into the history of the Connecticut Indians. The Pequots, he had discovered in a book that very afternoon, had been woefully incompetent fighters. Some early militarist had written of them that, fighting as they did, they "couldn't have killed seven people in seven years." They shot their arrows high into the air: anybody could see them coming and step out of the way. The Colonial militiamen used to pick up the flinted sticks, break them in two, and laugh at their helpless foes. Even when the shafts did get home, they almost never killed; a neckcloth would turn them aside or even, as in the case of one soldier, a piece of cheese carried in one's pocket. Poor, pathetic, stupid old Pequots! Brave they had undeniably been, but dumb. Mr. Bentley had suddenly a rather kindly feeling for the Pequots. And he had, at the same time, a new, belittling vision of that grand old lady, the first Cora: he saw her leisurely firing through a chink in the wall of her house, taking all afternoon to knock off nineteen Indians who had no chance against her, who stood on the edge of a clearing firing arrows wistfully into the sky until one of the white woman's blunderbuss slugs —a tenpenny nail or a harness buckle—struck them down. If only they had rushed her! If only one of them had been smart enough to light the end of an arrow and stick it burning in the roof of the Allyn house! They would have finished her off fast enough if they had ever got her outside! Mr. Bentley's heart beat faster and his eyes blinked brightly.

"What is it?" asked Mrs. Bentley, coming back into the room. Her husband looked so eager and pleased, sitting there.

"I was just thinking," he said.

Mr. Pinwither's preliminary report on the new letter was long and dull. Mr. Bentley tried to look interested: he knew better than to appear indifferent to any holy relic connected with the Great Cora.

"Cora's had such a day!" said Mrs. Bentley, as they were preparing for bed. "She went to sleep playing with those toy soldiers and Indians her Uncle Bert gave her." Mr. Bentley had one of his vivid pictures of Uncle Bert. "Um," he said, and went downstairs to get his aspirin box out of his coat.

Before he went to bed, Mr. Bentley stopped in the nursery to have a good-night look at his little sleeping daughter. She lay sweetly with her hands curled above her head. Mr. Bentley regarded the little girl with sad eyes. The line of her forehead and the curve of her chin were (or so the Allyns hysterically claimed) the unmistakable sign of the Great Cora, the proof of the child's proud heritage, the latest blaze along the trail. He stood above her, thinking, a long time.

When Mr. Bentley went back to the bedroom, it was pitch-dark; his wife had turned out the light. He tiptoed in. He heard her slow, deep breathing. She was sound asleep.

"Henry?" she called suddenly out of the blackness. Surprised, he did not answer.

"Henry!" she said. There was uneasiness and drowsy bewilderment in her voice.

To Henry Bentley, standing there in the darkness, there came a quick, wild urge. He tried to restrain it, and then, abruptly, he gave way to it, with a profound sense of release. Patting the fingers of his right hand rapidly against his open lips, he gave, at the top of his voice, the Pequot war whoop: "Ah-wah-wah-wah-wah!"

XII. The Private Life of Mr. Bidwell

From where she was sitting, Mrs. Bidwell could not see her husband, but she had a curious feeling of tension: she knew he was up to something.

"What are you doing, George?" she demanded, her eyes still on her book.

"Mm?"

"What's the matter with you?"

"Pahhhhh-h-h," said Mr. Bidwell, in a long, pleasurable exhale. "I was holding my breath."

Mrs. Bidwell twisted creakingly in her chair and looked at him; he was sitting behind her in his favorite place under the parchment lamp with the street scene of old New York on it. "I was just holding my breath," he said again.

"Well, please don't do it," said Mrs. Bidwell, and went back to her book. There was silence for five minutes.

"George!" said Mrs. Bidwell.

"Bwaaaaaa," said Mr. Bidwell. "What?"

"Will you please *stop* that?" she said. "It makes me nervous."

"I don't see how that bothers you," he said. "Can't I breathe?"

"You can breathe without holding your breath like a goop," said Mrs. Bidwell. "Goop" was a word that she was fond of using; she rather lazily applied it to everything. It annoyed Mr. Bidwell.

"Deep breathing," said Mr. Bidwell, in the impatient tone he used when explaining anything to his wife, "is good exercise. You ought to take more exercise."

"Well, please don't do it around me," said Mrs. Bidwell, turning again to the pages of Mr. Galsworthy.

At the Cowans' party, a week later, the room was full of chattering people when Mrs. Bidwell, who was talking to Lida Carroll, suddenly turned around as if she had been summoned. In a chair in a far corner of the room, Mr. Bidwell was holding his breath. His chest was expanded, his chin drawn in; there was a strange stare in his eyes, and his face was slightly empurpled. Mrs. Bidwell moved into the line of his vision and gave him a sharp, penetrating look. He deflated slowly and looked away.

Later, in the car, after they had driven in silence a mile or more on the way home, Mrs. Bidwell said, "It seems to me you might at least have the kindness not to hold your breath in other people's houses."

"I wasn't hurting anybody," said Mr. Bidwell.

"You looked silly!" said his wife. "You looked perfectly crazy!" She was driving and she began to speed up, as she always did when excited or angry. "What do you suppose people thought—you sitting there all swelled up, with your eyes popping out?"

"I wasn't all swelled up," he said, angrily.

"You looked like a goop," she said. The car slowed down, sighed, and came to a complete, despondent stop.

"We're out of gas," said Mrs. Bidwell. It was bitterly cold and nastily sleeting. Mr. Bidwell took a long, deep breath.

The breathing situation in the Bidwell family reached a critical point when Mr. Bidwell began to inhale in his sleep, slowly, and exhale with a protracted, growling "wooooooooo." Mrs. Bidwell, ordinarily a sound sleeper (except on nights when she was sure burglars were getting in), would wake up and reach over and shake her husband. "George!" she would say.

"Hawwwwww," Mr. Bidwell would say, thickly. "Wahs maa nah, hm?"

After he had turned over and gone back to sleep, Mrs. Bidwell would lie awake, thinking.

One morning at breakfast she said, "George, I'm not going to put up with this another day. If you can't stop blowing up like a grampus, I'm going to leave you." There was a slight, quick lift in Mr. Bidwell's heart, but he tried to look surprised and hurt.

"All right," he said. "Let's not talk about it."

Mrs. Bidwell buttered another piece of toast. She described to him the way he sounded in his sleep. He read the paper.

With considerable effort, Mr. Bidwell kept from inflating his chest for about a week, but one night at the McNally's he hit on the idea of seeing how many seconds he could hold his breath. He was rather bored by the McNally's party, anyway. He began timing himself with his wrist-watch in a remote corner of the living-room. Mrs. Bidwell, who was in the kitchen talking children and clothes with Bea McNally, left her abruptly and slipped back into the living-room. She stood quietly behind her husband's chair. He knew she was there, and tried to let out his breath imperceptibly.

"I see you," she said, in a low, cold tone. Mr. Bidwell jumped up.

"Why don't you let me alone?" he demanded.

"Will you please lower your voice?" she said, smiling so that if anyone were looking he wouldn't think the Bidwells were arguing.

"I'm getting pretty damned tired of this," said Bidwell in a low voice.

"You've ruined my evening!" she whispered.

"You've ruined mine, too!" he whispered back. They knifed each other, from head to stomach, with their eyes.

"Sitting here like a goop, holding your breath," said Mrs. Bidwell. "People will think you are an idiot." She laughed, turning to greet a lady who was approaching them.

Mr. Bidwell sat in his office the next afternoon, a black, moist afternoon, tapping a pencil on his desk, and scowling. "All right, then, get out, get out!" he muttered. "What do I care?" He was visualizing the scene when Mrs. Bidwell would walk out on him. After going through it several times, he returned to his work, feeling vaguely contented. He made up his mind to breathe any way he wanted to, no matter what she did. And, having come to this decision, he oddly enough, and quite without effort, lost interest in holding his breath.

Everything went rather smoothly at the Bidwells' for a month or so. Mr. Bidwell didn't do anything to annoy his wife beyond leaving his razor on her dressing-table and forgetting to turn out the hall light when he went to bed. Then there came the night of the Bentons' party.

Mr. Bidwell, bored as usual, was sitting in a far corner of the room, breathing normally. His wife was talking animatedly with Beth Williamson about negligees. Suddenly her voice slowed and an uneasy look came into her eyes: George was up to something. She turned around and sought him out. To anyone but Mrs. Bidwell he must have seemed like any husband sitting in a chair. But his wife's lips set tightly. She walked casually over to him.

"What are you doing?" she demanded.

"Hm?" he said, looking at her vacantly.

"What are you *doing*?" she demanded, again. He gave her a harsh, venomous look, which she returned.

"I'm multiplying numbers in my head," he said, slowly and evenly, "if you must know." In the prolonged, probing examination that they silently, without moving any muscles save those of their eyes, gave each other, it became solidly, frozenly apparent to both of them that the end of their endurance had arrived. The curious bond that held them together snapped— rather more easily than either had supposed was possible. That night, while undressing for bed, Mr. Bidwell calmly multiplied numbers in his head. Mrs. Bidwell stared coldly at him for a few moments, holding a stocking in her hand; she didn't bother to berate him. He paid no attention to her. The thing was simply over.

George Bidwell lives alone now (his wife remarried). He never goes to parties any more, and his old circle of friends rarely sees him. The last time that any of them did see him, he was walking along a country road with the halting, uncertain gait of a blind man: he was trying to see how many steps he could take without opening his eyes.

XIII. The Curb in the Sky

When Charlie Deshler announced that he was going to marry Dorothy, someone said he would lose his mind posthaste. "No," said a wit who knew them both, "post hoc." Dorothy had begun, when she was quite young, to finish sentences for people. Sometimes she finished them wrongly, which annoyed the person who was speaking, and sometimes she finished them correctly, which annoyed the speaker even more.

"When William Howard Taft was—" some guest in Dorothy's family's home would begin.

"President!" Dorothy would pipe up. The speaker may have meant to say "President" or he may have meant to say "young," or "Chief Justice of the Supreme Court of the United States." In any case, he would shortly put on his hat and go home. Like most parents, Dorothy's parents did not seem to be conscious that her mannerism was a nuisance. Very likely they thought that it was cute, or even bright. It is even probable that when Dorothy's mother first said "Come, Dorothy, eat your—" and Dorothy said "Spinach, dear," the former telephoned Dorothy's father at the office and told him about it, and he told everybody he met that day about it—and the next day and the day after.

When Dorothy grew up she became quite pretty and so even more of a menace. Gentlemen became attracted to her and then attached to her. Emotionally she stirred them, but mentally she soon began to wear them down. Even in her late teens she began correcting their English. "Not 'was,' Arthur," she would say, "'were.' 'Were prepared.' See?" Most of her admirers tolerated this habit because of their interest in her lovely person, but as time went on and her interest in them remained more instructive than sentimental, they slowly drifted away to less captious, if dumber, girls.

Charlie Deshler, however, was an impetuous man, of the sweep-them-off-their-feet persuasion, and he became engaged to Dorothy so quickly and married her in so short a time that, being deaf to the warnings of friends, whose concern he regarded as mere jealousy, he really didn't know anything about Dorothy except that she was pretty and bright-eyed and (to him) desirable.

Dorothy as a wife came, of course, into her great flowering: she took to correcting Charlie's stories. He had travelled widely and experienced greatly and was a truly excellent *raconteur*. Dorothy was, during their courtship, genuinely interested in him and in his stories, and since she had never shared any of the adventures he told about, she could not know when he made mistakes in time or in place or in identities. Beyond suggesting a change here and there in the number of a verb, she more or less let him alone. Charlie spoke rather good English, anyway—he knew when to say "were" and when to say "was" after "if"—and this was another reason he didn't find Dorothy out.

I didn't call on them for quite a while after they were married, because I liked Charlie and I knew I would feel low if I saw him coming out of the anesthetic of her charms and beginning to feel the first pains of reality. When I did finally call, conditions were, of course, all that I had feared. Charlie began to tell, at dinner, about a motor trip the two had made to this town and that—I never found out for sure what towns, because Dorothy denied almost everything that Charlie said. "The next day," he would say, "we got an early start and drove two hundred miles to Fairview—" "Well," Dorothy would say, "I wouldn't call it *early*. It wasn't as early as the first day we set out, when we got up about *seven*. And we only drove a hundred and eighty miles, because I remember looking at that mileage thing when we started."

"Anyway, when we got to Fairview—" Charlie would go on. But Dorothy would stop him. "Was it Fairview that day, darling?" she would ask. Dorothy often interrupted Charlie by asking him if he were right, instead of telling him that he was wrong, but it amounted to the same thing, for if he would reply: "Yes, I'm sure it was Fairview," she would say: "But it *wasn't*, darling," and then go on with the story herself. (She called everybody that she differed from "darling.")

Once or twice, when I called on them or they called on me, Dorothy would let Charlie get almost to the climax of some interesting account of a happening and then, like a tackler from behind, throw him just as he was about to cross the goal-line. There is nothing in life more shocking to the nerves and to the mind than this. Some husbands will sit back amiably—almost it seems, proudly—when their wives interrupt, and let them go on with the story, but these are beaten husbands. Charlie did not become beaten. But his wife's tackles knocked the wind out of him, and he began to realize that he would have to do something. What he did was rather ingenious. At the end of the second year of their marriage, when you visited the Deshlers, Charlie would begin some outlandish story about a dream

he had had, knowing that Dorothy could not correct him on his own dreams. They became the only life he had that was his own.

"I thought I was running an airplane," he would say, "made out of telephone wires and pieces of old leather. I was trying to make it fly to the moon, taking off from my bedroom. About halfway up to the moon, however, a man who looked like Santa Claus, only he was dressed in the uniform of a customs officer, waved at me to stop—he was in a plane made of telephone wires, too. So I pulled over to a cloud. 'Here,' he said to me, 'you can't go to the moon, if you are the man who invented these wedding cookies.' Then he showed me a cookie made in the shape of a man and woman being married—little images of a man and a woman and a minister, made of dough and fastened firmly to a round, crisp cookie base." So he would go on.

Any psychiatrist will tell you that at the end of the way Charlie was going lies madness in the form of monomania. You can't live in a fantastic dream world, night in and night out and then day in and day out, and remain sane. The substance began to die slowly out of Charlie's life, and he began to live entirely in shadow. And since monomania of this sort is likely to lead in the end to the reiteration of one particular story, Charlie's invention began to grow thin and he eventually took to telling, over and over again, the first dream he had ever described—the story of his curious flight toward the moon in an airplane made of telephone wires. It was extremely painful. It saddened us all.

After a month or two, Charlie finally had to be sent to an asylum. I was out of town when they took him away, but Joe Fultz, who went with him, wrote me about it. "He seemed to like it up here right away," Joe wrote. "He's calmer and his eyes look better." (Charlie had developed a wild, hunted look.) "Of course," concluded Joe, "he's finally got away from that woman."

It was a couple of weeks later that I drove up to the asylum to see Charlie. He was lying on a cot on a big screened-in porch, looking wan and thin. Dorothy was sitting on a chair beside his bed, bright-eyed and eager. I was somehow surprised to see her there, having figured that Charlie had, at least, won sanctuary from his wife. He looked quite mad. He began at once to tell me the story of his trip to the moon. He got to the part where the man who looked like Santa Claus waved at him to stop. "He was in a plane made of telephone wires, too," said Charlie. "So I pulled over to a curb——"

"No. You pulled over to a *cloud*," said Dorothy. "There aren't any curbs in the *sky*. There *couldn't* be. You pulled over to a cloud."

Charlie sighed and turned slightly in his bed and looked at me. Dorothy looked at me, too, with her pretty smile.

"He always gets that story wrong," she said.

XIV. Mr. Preble Gets Rid of His Wife

Mr. Preble was a plump middle-aged lawyer in Scarsdale. He used to kid with his stenographer about running away with him. "Let's run away together," he would say, during a pause in dictation. "All righty," she would say.

One rainy Monday afternoon, Mr. Preble was more serious about it than usual.

"Let's run away together," said Mr. Preble.

"All righty," said his stenographer. Mr. Preble jingled the keys in his pocket and looked out the window.

"My wife would be glad to get rid of me," he said.

"Would she give you a divorce?" asked the stenographer.

"I don't suppose so," he said. The stenographer laughed.

"You'd have to get rid of your wife," she said.

Mr. Preble was unusually silent at dinner that night. About half an hour after coffee, he spoke without looking up from his paper.

"Let's go down in the cellar," Mr. Preble said to his wife.

"What for?" she said, not looking up from her book.

"Oh, I don't know," he said. "We never go down in the cellar any more. The way we used to."

"We never did go down in the cellar that I remember," said Mrs. Preble. "I could rest easy the balance of my life if I never went down in the cellar." Mr. Preble was silent for several minutes.

"Supposing I said it meant a whole lot to me," began Mr. Preble.

"What's come over you?" his wife demanded. "It's cold down there and there is absolutely nothing to do."

"We could pick up pieces of coal," said Mr. Preble. "We might get up some kind of a game with pieces of coal."

"I don't want to," said his wife. "Anyway, I'm reading."

"Listen," said Mr. Preble, rising and walking up and down. "Why won't you come down in the cellar? You can read down there, as far as that goes."

"There isn't a good enough light down there," she said, "and anyway, I'm not going to go down in the cellar. You may as well make up your mind to that."

"Gee whiz!" said Mr. Preble, kicking at the edge of a rug. "Other people's wives go down in the cellar. Why is it you never want to do anything? I come home worn out from the office and you won't even go down in the cellar with me. God knows it isn't very far—it isn't as if I was asking you to go to the movies or some place."

"I don't want to *go!*" shouted Mrs. Preble. Mr. Preble sat down on the edge of a davenport.

"All right, all *right*," he said. He picked up the newspaper again. "I wish you'd let me tell you more about it. It's—kind of a surprise."

"Will you quit harping on that subject?" asked Mrs. Preble.

"Listen," said Mr. Preble, leaping to his feet. "I might as well

tell you the truth instead of beating around the bush. I want to get rid of you so I can marry my stenographer. Is there anything especially wrong about that? People do it every day. Love is something you can't control——"

"We've been all over that," said Mrs. Preble. "I'm not going to go all over that again."

"I just wanted you to know how things are," said Mr. Preble. "But you have to take everything so literally. Good Lord, do you suppose I really wanted to go down in the cellar and make up some silly game with pieces of coal?"

"I never believed that for a minute," said Mrs. Preble. "I knew all along you wanted to get me down there and bury me."

"You can say that now—after I told you," said Mr. Preble. "But it would never have occurred to you if I hadn't."

"You didn't tell me; I got it out of you," said Mrs. Preble. "Anyway, I'm always two steps ahead of what you're thinking."

"You're never within a mile of what I'm thinking," said Mr. Preble.

"Is that so? I knew you wanted to bury me the minute you set foot in this house tonight." Mrs. Preble held him with a glare.

"Now that's just plain damn exaggeration," said Mr. Preble, considerably annoyed. "You knew nothing of the sort. As a matter of fact, I never thought of it till just a few minutes ago."

"It was in the back of your mind," said Mrs. Preble. "I suppose this filing woman put you up to it."

"You needn't get sarcastic," said Mr. Preble. "I have plenty of people to file without having her file. She doesn't know anything about this. She isn't in on it. I was going to tell her you had gone to visit some friends and fell over a cliff. She wants me to get a divorce."

"That's a laugh," said Mrs. Preble. "*That's* a laugh. You may bury me, but you'll never get a divorce."

"She knows that! I told her that," said Mr. Preble. "I mean —I told her I'd never get a divorce."

"Oh, you probably told her about burying me, too," said Mrs. Preble.

"That's not true," said Mr. Preble, with dignity. "That's between you and me. I was never going to tell a soul."

"You'd blab it to the whole world; don't tell me," said Mrs. Preble. "I know you." Mr. Preble puffed at his cigar.

"I wish you were buried now and it was all over with," he said.

"Don't you suppose you would get caught, you crazy thing?" she said. "They always get caught. Why don't you go to bed? You're just getting yourself all worked up over nothing."

"I'm not going to bed," said Mr. Preble. "I'm going to bury you in the cellar. I've got my mind made up to it. I don't know how I could make it any plainer."

"Listen," cried Mrs. Preble, throwing her book down, "will you be satisfied and shut up if I go down in the cellar? Can I have a little peace if I go down in the cellar? Will you let me alone then?"

"Yes," said Mr. Preble. "But you spoil it by taking that attitude."

"Sure, sure, I always spoil everything. I stop reading right in the middle of a chapter. I'll never know how the story comes out—but that's nothing to you."

"Did I make you start reading the book?" asked Mr. Preble. He opened the cellar door. "Here, you go first."

"Brrr," said Mrs. Preble, starting down the steps. "It's *cold* down here! You *would* think of this, at this time of year! Any other husband would have buried his wife in the summer."

"You can't arrange those things just whenever you want to,"

said Mr. Preble. "I didn't fall in love with this girl till late fall."

"Anybody else would have fallen in love with her long before that. She's been around for years. Why is it you always let other men get in ahead of you? Mercy, but it's dirty down here! What have you got there?"

"I was going to hit you over the head with this shovel," said Mr. Preble.

"You were, huh?" said Mrs. Preble. "Well, get that out of your mind. Do you want to leave a great big clue right here in the middle of everything where the first detective that comes snooping around will find it? Go out in the street and find some piece of iron or something—something that doesn't belong to you."

"Oh, all right," said Mr. Preble. "But there won't be any piece of iron in the street. Women always expect to pick up a piece of iron anywhere."

"If you look in the right place you'll find it," said Mrs. Preble. "And don't be gone long. Don't you dare stop in at the cigarstore. I'm not going to stand down here in this cold cellar all night and freeze."

"All right," said Mr. Preble. "I'll hurry."

"And shut that *door* behind you!" she screamed after him. "Where were you born—in a barn?"

XV. A Portrait of Aunt Ida

My mother's Aunt Ida Clemmens died the other day out West. She was ninety-one years old. I remember her clearly, although I haven't thought about her in a long time and never saw her after I was twenty. I remember how dearly she loved catastrophes, especially those of a national or international importance. The sinking of the *Titanic* was perhaps the most important tragedy of the years in which I knew her. She never saw in such things, as her older sisters, Emma and Clara, did, the vengeance of a Deity outraged by Man's lust for speed and gaiety; she looked for the causes deep down in the dark heart of the corporate interests. You could never make her believe that the *Titanic* hit an iceberg. Whoever *heard* of such a thing! It was simply a flimsy prevarication devised to cover up the real cause. The real cause she could not, or would not, make plain, but somewhere in its black core was a monstrous secret of treachery and corrupt goings-on—men were like that. She came later on to doubt the courage of the brave gentlemen on the sinking ship who at the last waved goodbye smilingly and smoked cigarettes. It was her growing conviction that most of them had to be shot by the ship's officers in order to prevent them from crowding into the lifeboats ahead of the older and less attractive women passengers. Eminence and wealth in men Aunt Ida persistently attributed to deceit, trickery, and impiety. I think the only famous person she ever trusted in her time was President McKinley.

The disappearance of Judge Crater, the Hall-Mills murder, the Starr Faithfull case, and similar mysteries must have made Aunt Ida's last years happy. She loved the unsolvable and the unsolved. Mysteries that were never cleared up were brought about, in her opinion, by the workings of some strange force in the world which we do not thoroughly understand and which God does not intend that we ever shall understand. An invisible power, a power akin to electricity and radio (both of which she must have regarded as somehow or other blasphemous), but never to be isolated or channelled. Out of this power came murder, disappearances, and supernatural phenomena. All persons connected in any way whatever with celebrated cases were tainted in Aunt Ida's sight—and that went for prosecuting attorneys, too (always "tricky" men). But she would, I'm sure, rather have had a look at Willie Stevens than at President Roosevelt, at Jafsie than at the King of England, just as she would rather have gone through the old Wendel house than the White House.

Surgical operations and post-mortems were among Aunt Ida's special interests, although she did not believe that any operation was ever necessary and she was convinced that post-mortems were conducted to cover up something rather than to find something out. It was her conviction that doctors were in the habit of trying to obfuscate or distort the true facts about illness and death. She believed that many of her friends and relatives had been laid away without the real causes of their deaths being entered on the "city books." She was fond of telling a long and involved story about the death of one of her first cousins, a married woman who had passed away at twenty-five. Aunt Ida for thirty years contended that there was something "behind it." She believed that a certain physician, a gentleman of the highest reputation, would some day "tell the truth about Ruth," perhaps on his deathbed. When he died (without confessing, of course), she said after reading the account in the newspaper that she had dreamed of him a few nights before. It seemed that he had called to her and wanted to tell her something but couldn't.

Aunt Ida believed that she was terribly psychic. She had warnings, premonitions, and "feelings." They were invariably intimations of approaching misfortune, sickness, or death. She never had a premonition that everything was going to be all right. It was always that Grace So-and-So was not going to marry the man she was engaged to, or that Mr. Hollowell, who was down in South America on business, would never return, or that old Mrs. Hutchins would not last out the year (she missed on old Mrs. Hutchins for twenty-two years but finally made it). Most all of Aunt Ida's forewarnings of financial ruin and marital tragedy came in the daytime while she was marketing or sitting hulling peas; most all of her intimations of death appeared to her in dreams. Dreams of Ohio women of Aunt Ida's generation were never Freudian; they were purely prophetic. They dealt with black hearses and white hearses rolling soundlessly along through the night, and with coffins being carried out of houses, and with tombstones bearing names and dates, and with tall, faceless women in black veils and gloves. Most of Aunt Ida's dreams foretold the fate of women, for what happened to women was of much greater importance to Aunt Ida than what happened to men. Men usually "brought things on themselves"; women, on the other

hand, were usually the victims of dark and devious goings-on of a more or less supernatural nature.

Birth was, in some ways, as dark a matter to Aunt Ida as death. She felt that most babies, no matter what you said or anybody else said, were "not wanted." She believed that the children of famous people, brilliant people, and of first, second, or third cousins would be idiotic. If a child died young, she laid it to the child's parentage, no matter what the immediate cause of death might have been. "There is something in that family," Aunt Ida used to say, in her best funeral voice. This something was a vague, ominous thing, both far off and close at hand, misty and ready to spring, compounded of nobody could guess exactly what. One of Aunt Ida's favorite predictions was "They'll never raise that baby, you mark my words." The fact that they usually did never shook her confidence in her "feelings." If she was right once in twenty times, it proved that she knew what she was talking about. In foretelling the sex of unborn children, she was right about half the time.

Life after death was a source of speculation, worry, and exhilaration to Aunt Ida. She firmly believed that people could "come back" and she could tell you of many a house that was haunted (barrels of apples rolled down the attic steps of one of them, I remember, but it was never clear why they did). Aunt Ida put no faith in mediums or séances. The dead preferred to come back to the houses where they had lived and to go stalking through the rooms and down the halls. I think Aunt Ida always thought of them as coming back in the flesh, fully clothed, for she always spoke of them as "the dead," never as ghosts. The reason they came back was that they had left something unsaid or undone that must be corrected. Although a descendant of staunch orthodox Methodists, some of them ministers, Aunt Ida in her later years dabbled a little in various religions, superstitions, and even cults. She found astrology, New Thought, and the theory of reincarnation comforting. The people who are bowed down in this life, she grew to believe, will have another chance.

Aunt Ida was confident that the world was going to be destroyed almost any day. When Halley's comet appeared in 1910, she expected to read in the papers every time she picked them up the news that Paris had gone up in flames and that New York City had slid into the ocean. Those two cities, being horrible dens of vice, were bound to go first; the smaller towns would be destroyed in a more leisurely fashion with some respectable and dignified ending for the pious and the kindly people.

Two of Aunt Ida's favorite expressions were "I never heard of such a thing" and "If I never get up from this chair. . . ." She told all stories of death, misfortune, grief, corruption, and disaster with vehemence and exaggeration. She was hampered in narration by her inability to think of names, particularly simple names, such as Joe, Earl, Ned, Harry, Louise, Ruth, Bert. Somebody usually had to prompt her with the name of the third cousin, or whomever, that she was trying to think of, but she was unerring in her ability to remember difficult names the rest of us had long forgotten. "He used to work in the old Schirtzberger & Wallenheim saddle store in Naughton Street," she would say. "What *was* his name?" It would turn out that his name was Frank Butler.

Up to the end, they tell me, Aunt Ida could read without her glasses, and none of the commoner frailties of senility affected her. She had no persecution complex, no lapses of memory, no trailing off into the past, no unfounded bitternesses—unless you could call her violent hatred of cigarettes unfounded bitterness, and I don't think it was, because she actually knew stories of young men and even young women who had become paralyzed to the point of losing the use of both legs through smoking cigarettes. She tended to her begonias and wrote out a check for the rent the day she took to her bed for the last time. It irked her not to be up and about, and she accused the doctor the family brought in of not knowing his business. There was marketing to do, and friends to call on, and work to get through with. When friends and relatives began calling on her, she was annoyed. Making out that she was really sick! Old Mrs. Kurtz, who is seventy-two, visited her on the last day, and when she left, Aunt Ida looked after her pityingly. "Poor Cora," she said, "she's failin', ain't she?"

XVI. The Luck of Jad Peters

AUNT EMMA PETERS, at eighty-three—the year she died—still kept in her unused front parlor, on the table with Jad Peters's collection of lucky souvenirs, a large rough fragment of rock weighing perhaps twenty pounds. The rock stood in the centre of a curious array of odds and ends: a piece of tent canvas, a chip of pine wood, a yellowed telegram, some old newspaper clippings, the cork from a bottle, a bill from a surgeon. Aunt Emma never talked about the strange collection except once, during her last days, when somebody asked her if she wouldn't feel better if the rock were thrown away. "Let it stay where Lisbeth put it," she said. All that I know about the souvenirs I have got from other members of the family. A few of them didn't think it was "decent" that the rock should have been part of the collection, but Aunt Lisbeth, Emma's sister, had insisted that it should be. In fact, it was Aunt Lisbeth Banks who hired a man to lug it to the house and put it on the table with the rest of the things. "It's as much God's doing as that other clutter-trap," she would say. And she would rock back and forth in her rocking chair with a grim look. "You can't taunt the Lord," she would add. She was a very religious woman. I used to see her now and again at funerals, tall, gaunt, grim, but I never talked to her if I could help it. She liked funerals and she liked to look at corpses, and that made me afraid of her.

Just back of the souvenir table at Aunt Emma's, on the wall, hung a heavy-framed, full-length photograph of Aunt Emma's husband, Jad Peters. It showed him wearing a hat and overcoat and carrying a suitcase. When I was a little boy in the early nineteen-hundreds and was taken to Aunt Emma's house near Sugar Grove, Ohio, I used to wonder about that photograph (I didn't wonder about the rock and the other objects, because they weren't put there till much later). It seemed so funny for anyone to be photographed in a hat and overcoat and carrying a suitcase, and even funnier to have the photograph enlarged to almost life size and put inside so elaborate a frame. When we children would sneak into the front parlor to look at the picture, Aunt Emma would hurry us out again. When we asked her about the picture, she would say, "Never you mind." But when I grew up, I learned the story of the big photograph and of how Jad Peters came to be known as Lucky Jad. As a matter of fact, it was Jad who began calling himself that; once when he ran for a county office (and lost) he had "Lucky Jad Peters" printed on his campaign cards. Nobody else took the name up except in a scoffing way.

It seems that back in 1888, when Jad Peters was about thirty five, he had a pretty good business of some kind or other which caused him to travel around quite a lot. One week he went to New York with the intention of going on to Newport, later, by ship. Something turned up back home, however, and one of his employees sent him a telegram reading "Don't go to

Newport. Urgent you return here." Jad's story was that he was on the ship, ready to sail, when the telegram was delivered; it had been sent to his hotel, he said, a few minutes after he had checked out, and an obliging clerk had hustled the messenger boy on down to the dock. That was Jad's story. Most people believed, when they heard the story, that Jad had got the wire at his hotel, probably hours before the ship sailed, for he was a great one at adorning a tale. At any rate, whether or not he rushed off the ship just before the gangplank was hauled up, it sailed without him and some eight or nine hours out of the harbor sank in a storm with the loss of everybody on board. That's why he had the photograph taken and enlarged: it showed him just as he was when he got off the ship, he said. And that is how he came to start his collection of lucky souvenirs. For a few years he kept the telegram, and newspaper clippings of the ship disaster, tucked away in the family Bible, but one day he got them out and put them on the parlor table under a big glass bell.

From 1888 up until 1920, when Jad died, nothing much happened to him. He is remembered in his later years as a garrulous, boring old fellow whose business slowly went to pieces because of his lack of industry and who finally settled down on a small farm near Sugar Grove and barely scraped out an existence. He took to drinking in his sixties, and from then on made Aunt Emma's life miserable. I don't know how she managed to keep up the payments on his life-insurance policy, but some way or other she did. Some of her relatives said among themselves that it would be a blessing if Jad died in one of his frequent fits of nausea. It was pretty well known that Aunt Emma had never liked him very much—she married him because he asked her to twice a week for seven years and because there had been nobody else she cared about; she stayed married to him on account of their children and because her people always stayed married. She grew, in spite of Jad, to be

a quiet, kindly old lady as the years went on, although her mouth would take on a strained, tight look when Jad showed up at dinner time from wherever he had been during the day —usually from down at Prentice's store in the village, where he liked to sit around telling about the time he just barely got off the doomed boat in New York harbor in '88 and adding tales, more or less fantastic, of more recent close escapes he had had. There was his appendicitis operation, for one thing: he had come out of the ether, he would say, just when they had given him up. Dr. Benham, who had performed the operation, was annoyed when he heard this, and once met Jad in the street and asked him to quit repeating the preposterous story, but Jad added the doctor's bill to his collection of talismans, anyway. And there was the time when he had got up in the night to take a swig of stomach bitters for a bad case of heart-burn and had got hold of the carbolic-acid bottle by mistake. Something told him, he would say, to take a look at the bottle before he uncorked it, so he carried it to a lamp, lighted the lamp, and he'd be gol-dam if it wasn't carbolic acid! It was then that he added the cork to his collection.

Old Jad got so that he could figure out lucky escapes for himself in almost every disaster and calamity that happened in and around Sugar Grove. Once, for example, a tent blew down during a wind storm at the Fairfield County Fair, killing two people and injuring a dozen others. Jad hadn't gone to the fair that year for the first time in nine or ten years. Something told him, he would say, to stay away from the fair that year. The fact that he always went to the fair, when he did go, on a Thursday and that the tent blew down on a Saturday didn't make any difference to Jad. He hadn't been there and the tent blew down and two people were killed. After the accident, he went to the fair grounds and cut a piece of canvas from the tent and put it on the parlor table next to the cork from the carbolic-acid bottle. Lucky Jad Peters!

I think Aunt Emma got so that she didn't hear Jad when he was talking, except on evenings when neighbors dropped in, and then she would have to take hold of the conversation and steer it away from any opening that might give Jad a chance to tell of some close escape he had had. But he always got his licks in. He would bide his time, creaking back and forth in his chair, clicking his teeth, and not listening much to the talk about crops and begonias and the latest reports on the Spencers' feeble-minded child, and then, when there was a long pause, he would clear his throat and say that that reminded him of the time he had had a mind to go down to Pullen's lumber yard to fetch home a couple of two-by-fours to shore up the chicken house. Well, sir, he had pottered around the house a little while and was about to set out for Pullen's when something told him not to go a step. And it was that very day that a pile of lumber in the lumber yard let go and crushed Grant Pullen's leg so's it had to be amputated. Well, sir, he would say—but Aunt Emma would cut in on him at this point. "Everybody's heard that old chestnut," she would say, with a forced little laugh, fanning herself in quick strokes with an old palm-leaf fan. Jad would go sullen and rock back and forth in his chair, clicking his teeth. He wouldn't get up when the guests rose to go—which they always did at this juncture. The memento of his close escape from the Pullen lumber-yard disaster was, of course, the chip of pine wood.

I think I have accounted for all of Jad's souvenirs that I remember except the big rough fragment of rock. The story of the rock is a strange one. In August, 1920, county engineers were widening the channel of the Hocking River just outside of Sugar Grove and had occasion to do considerable blasting out of river-bed rock. I have never heard Clem Warden tell the story himself, but it has been told to me by people who have. It seems that Clem was walking along the main street of

Sugar Grove at about a quarter to four when he saw Jad coming along toward him. Clem was an old crony of Jad's—one of the few men of his own generation who could tolerate Jad —and the two stopped on the sidewalk and talked. Clem figured later that they had talked for about five minutes, and then either he or Jad said something about getting on, so they separated, Jad going on toward Prentice's store, slowly, on account of his rheumatic left hip, and Clem going in the other direction. Clem had taken about a dozen steps when suddenly he heard Jad call to him. "Say, Clem!" Jad said. Clem stopped and turned around, and here was Jad walking back toward him. Jad had taken about six steps when suddenly he was flung up against the front of Matheny's harness store "like a sack o' salt," as Clem put it. By the time Clem could reach him, he was gone. He never knew what hit him, Clem said, and for quite a few minutes nobody else knew what hit him, either. Then somebody in the crowd that gathered found the big muddy rock lying in the road by the gutter. A particularly big shot of dynamite, set off in the river bed, had hurtled the fragment through the air with terrific force. It had come flying over the four-story Jackson Building like a cannon ball and had struck Jad Peters squarely in the chest.

I suppose old Jad hadn't been in his grave two days before the boys at Prentice's quit shaking their heads solemnly over the accident and began making funny remarks about it. Cal Gregg's was the funniest. "Well, sir," said Cal, "I don't suppose none of us will ever know what it was now, but somethin' must of told Jad to turn around."

XVII. I Went to Sullivant

I WAS reminded the other morning—by what, I don't remember and it doesn't matter—of a crisp September morning last year when I went to the Grand Central to see a little boy of ten get excitedly on a special coach that was to take him to a boys' school somewhere north of Boston. He had never been away to school before. The coach was squirming with youngsters; you could tell, after a while, the novitiates, shining and tremulous and a little awed, from the more aloof boys, who had been away to school before, but they were all very much alike at first glance. There was for me (in case you thought I was leading up to that) no sharp feeling of old lost years in the tense atmosphere of that coach, because I never went away to a private school when I was a little boy. I went to Sullivant School in Columbus. I thought about it as I walked back to my hotel.

Sullivant was an ordinary public school, and yet it was not like any other I have ever known of. In seeking an adjective to describe the Sullivant School of my years—1900 to 1908—

I can only think of "tough." Sullivant School was tough. The boys of Sullivant came mostly from the region around Central Market, a poorish district with many colored families and many white families of the laboring class. The school district also included a number of homes of the upper classes because, at the turn of the century, one or two old residential streets still lingered near the shouting and rumbling of the market, reluctant to surrender their fine old houses to the encroaching rabble of commerce, and become (as, alas, they now have) mere vulgar business streets.

I remember always, first of all, the Sullivant baseball team. Most grammar-school baseball teams are made up of boys in the seventh and eighth grades, or they were in my day, but with Sullivant it was different. Several of its best players were in the fourth grade, known to the teachers of the school as the Terrible Fourth. In that grade you first encountered fractions and long division, and many pupils lodged there for years, like logs in a brook. Some of the more able baseball-players had been in the fourth grade for seven or eight years. Then, too, there were a number of boys, most of them colored (about half of the pupils at Sullivant were colored), who had not been in the class past the normal time but were nevertheless deep in their teens. They had avoided starting to school—by eluding the truant officer—until they were ready to go into long pants, but he always got them in the end. One or two of these fourth-graders were seventeen or eighteen years old, but the dean of the squad was a tall, husky young man of twenty-two who was in the fifth grade (the teachers of the third and fourth had got tired of having him around as the years rolled along and had pushed him on). His name was Dana Waney and he had a mustache. Don't ask me why his parents allowed him to stay in school so long. There were many mysteries at Sullivant that were never cleared up. All I know is why he kept on in school and didn't go to work: he liked playing on the baseball team, and he had a pretty easy

time in class, because the teachers had given up asking him any questions at all years before. The story was that he had answered but one question in the seventeen years he had been going to classes at Sullivant and that was "What is one use of the comma?" "The commy," said Dana, embarrassedly unsnarling his long legs from beneath a desk much too low for him, "is used to shoot marbles with." ("Commies" was our word for those cheap, ten-for-a-cent marbles, in case it wasn't yours.)

The Sullivant School baseball team of 1905 defeated several high-school teams in the city and claimed the high-school championship of the state, to which title it had, of course, no technical right. I believe the boys could have proved their moral right to the championship, however, if they had been allowed to go out of town and play all the teams they challenged, such as the powerful Dayton and Toledo nines, but their road season was called off after a terrific fight that occurred during a game in Mt. Sterling, or Piqua, or Zenia—I can't remember which. Our first baseman—Dana Waney—crowned the umpire with a bat during an altercation over a called strike and the fight was on. It took place in the fourth inning, so of course the game was never finished (the battle continued on down into the business section of the town and raged for hours, with much destruction of property), but since Sullivant was ahead at the time 17 to 0 there could have been no doubt as to the outcome. Nobody was killed. All of us boys were sure our team could have beaten Ohio State University that year, but they wouldn't play us; they were scared.

Waney was by no means the biggest or toughest guy on the grammar-school team; he was merely the oldest, being about a year the senior of Floyd, the colored centre-fielder, who could jump five feet straight into the air without taking a running start. Nobody knew—not even the Board of Education, which once tried to find out—whether Floyd was Floyd's first name or his last name. He apparently only had one. He didn't have any parents, and nobody, including himself, seemed to know where he lived. When teachers insisted that he must have another name to go with Floyd, he would grow sullen and ominous and they would cease questioning him, because he was a dangerous scholar in a schoolroom brawl, as Mr. Harrigan, the janitor, found out one morning when he was called in by a screaming teacher (all our teachers were women) to get Floyd under control after she had tried to whip him and he had begun to take the room apart, beginning with the desks. Floyd broke into small pieces the switch she had used on him (some said he also ate it; I don't know, because I was home sick at the time with mumps or something). Harrigan was a burly, iron-muscled janitor, a man come from a long line of coal-shovellers, but he was no match for Floyd, who had, to be sure, the considerable advantage of being more aroused than Mr. Harrigan when their fight started. Floyd had him down and was sitting on his chest in no time, and Harrigan had to promise to be good and to say "Dat's what Ah get" ten times before Floyd would let him up.

I don't suppose I would ever have got through Sullivant School alive if it hadn't been for Floyd. For some reason he appointed himself my protector, and I needed one. If Floyd was known to be on your side, nobody in the school would dare be "after" you and chase you home. I was one of the ten or fifteen male pupils in Sullivant School who always, or almost always, knew their lessons, and I believe Floyd admired the mental prowess of a youngster who knew how many continents there were and whether or not the sun was inhabited. Also, one time when it came my turn to read to the class—we used to take turns reading American history aloud—I came across the word "Duquesne" and knew how to pronounce it. That charmed Floyd, who had been slouched in his seat idly following the printed page of his worn and pencilled textbook. "How you know dat was Dukane, boy?" he asked me after class. "I don't

know," I said. "I just knew it." He looked at me with round eyes. "Boy, dat's sump'n," he said. After that, word got around that Floyd would beat the tar out of anybody that messed around me. I wore glasses from the time I was eight and I knew my lessons, and both of those things were considered pretty terrible at Sullivant. Floyd had one idiosyncrasy. In the early nineteen-hundreds, long warm furry gloves that came almost to your elbows were popular with boys, and Floyd had one of the biggest pairs in school. He wore them the year around.

Dick Peterson, another colored boy, was an even greater figure on the baseball team and in the school than Floyd was. He had a way in the classroom of blurting out a long deep rolling "beee—eee—ahhhh!" for no reason at all. Once he licked three boys his own size single-handed, really single-handed, for he fought with his right hand and held a mandolin in his left hand all the time. It came out uninjured. Dick and Floyd never met in mortal combat, so nobody ever knew which one could "beat," and the scholars were about evenly divided in their opinions. Many a fight started among them after school when that argument came up. I think school never let out at Sullivant without at least one fight starting up, and sometimes there were as many as five or six raging between the corner of Oak and Sixth Streets and the corner of Rich and Fourth Streets, four blocks away. Now and again virtually the whole school turned out to fight the Catholic boys of the Holy Cross Academy in Fifth Street near Town, for no reason at all—in winter with snowballs and iceballs, in other seasons with fists, brickbats, and clubs. Dick Peterson was always in the van, yelling, singing, beeee-ahing, whirling all the way around when he swung with his right or (if he hadn't brought his mandolin) his left and missed. He made himself the pitcher on the baseball team because he was the captain. He was the captain because everybody was afraid to challenge his self-election, except Floyd. Floyd was too lazy to pitch and he didn't care who was captain, because he didn't fully comprehend what that meant. On one occasion, when Earl Battec, a steam-fitter's son, had shut out Mound Street School for six innings without a hit, Dick took him out of the pitcher's box and went in himself. He was hit hard and the other team scored, but it didn't make much difference, because the margin of Sullivant's victory was so great. The team didn't lose a game for five years to another grammar school. When Dick Peterson was in the sixth grade, he got into a saloon brawl and was killed.

When I go back to Columbus I always walk past Sullivant School. I have never happened to get there when classes were letting out, so I don't know what the pupils are like now. I am sure there are no more Dick Petersons and no more Floyds, unless Floyd is still going to school there. The play yard is still entirely bare of grass and covered with gravel, and the sycamores still line the curb between the schoolhouse fence and the Oak Street car line. A street-car line running past a schoolhouse is a dangerous thing as a rule, but I remember no one being injured while I was attending Sullivant. I do remember, however, one person who came very near being injured. He was a motorman on the Oak Street line, and once when his car stopped at the corner of Sixth to let off passengers, he yelled at Chutey Davidson, who played third base on the ball team, and was a member of the Terrible Fourth, to get out of the way. Chutey was a white boy, fourteen years old, but huge for his age, and he was standing on the tracks, taking a chew of tobacco. "Come ahn down offa that car an' I'll knock your block off!" said Chutey, in what I can only describe as a Sullivant tone of voice. The motorman waited until Chutey moved slowly off the tracks; then he went on about his business. I think it was lucky for him that he did. There were boys in those days.

XVIII. The Civil War Phone-Number Association

Mr. Rudy Vallée, in an interview (or maybe it was in an article), has said that sometimes when he goes backstage he is saddened at the sight of the members of his band sitting around reading detective stories. "They should try to improve their memories," says Mr. Vallée, "by associating telephone numbers, for instance, with the date of the Civil War."

This remarkable statement can be picked to pieces by any skillful Civil War telephone-number associator. In the first place, the use of the phrase "for instance" in the position we find it implies that Mr. Vallée thinks it is a good idea to sit around associating *various* things with the date of the Civil War ("telephone numbers, for instance"). Such a practice would confound even Salo Finkelstein, the lightning calculator. If a person has put in the afternoon associating his bank balance, his automobile license plates, and the total amount of his debts with the date of the Civil War, he is not going to be able to call up a phone number when he wants to; he is going to call up the money he has in the bank or the number on the back of his car. In the second place, it is futile to sit around, backstage or anywhere else, merely associating telephone numbers with the date of the Civil War and not calling anybody up. The purpose of the War of the Rebellion system of remembering phone numbers is not to keep them in the forefront of the mind, whence they can be brought up and recited to oneself as if they were limericks, but to tuck them away in the back of the mind, whence they can be called forth when needed and used for the practical purpose of getting in touch with somebody.

And in the third place, I must, as one of the oldest surviving veterans of the Civil War Telephone-Number Association, take firm exception to the expression "the date of the Civil War." The Civil War was full of dates, many of them—such as September 19, the date of the Battle of Chickamauga—as important and helpful as the war years themselves. Mr. Vallée's "date" would seem to indicate that he goes simply by 1861, the year the war began, or 1865, the year it ended. These would be useful in fixing in one's mind only about half a dozen numbers, such as Bryant 9-1861, Wickersham 2-1865, maybe Watkins 9-1961 (if you remember to subtract a hundred years), and possibly Gramercy 7-5681. This last is, of course, 1865 backward and seems simple; but in a phone booth, without a pencil, one could call up practically everybody in the south-central part of town without getting the right party, unless one were very good at visualizing four digits backward.

If I were Mr. Vallée and knew only one date for the Civil War, I should certainly give up the whole system of association and write the numbers I wanted to remember in a small book and carry it about with me. Even I, who know dozens of Civil War dates, including the hour of day that Stonewall Jackson was shot, sometimes wish I had gone in for the "jotting down" system. Using that method, if you get mad at somebody, you

can cross out his number in the little notebook and be quit of it, whereas if you have it filed away in your mind alongside of Pickett's charge, it is there ineradicably. I still know the phone number of a girl who gave me the go-by in 1920, and now and then, as the years roll away, it flicks around the back of my head annoyingly, like a deer fly, upsetting my day. The phone number of the American Embassy in Paris, for which I no longer have any possible use, often keeps me awake at night: Passy 12 . 50. Particularly on trains: Passy douze cinquante, Passy douze cinquante, chant the iron wheels on the rails.

It was eight years ago that I began to go in for associating telephone numbers with troop movements, in a big way. At that time, which was before the fifth digit got into Manhattan phone numbers and made my life and Mr. Vallée's even harder than they had been, my telephone number was Algonquin 9618. For some reason, that was hard for me. The Civil War fell down, in this case, almost completely, for although there was '61 in the middle to remember it by, the 9 and the 8 didn't seem to mean much. It was then that I began to toy with other wars, the war with Spain naturally (and unfortunately) suggesting itself because of 98. As a result, I would phone 9861 and then 6198 and in the end go completely to pieces and try all the permutations until I had run the entire gamut of numbers in the Algonquin exchange, from 1689, the lowest, to 9861, the highest. For an old war associator to quit fiddling his life away in a phone booth and look up his number in the directory would be, of course, an unthinkable defeat that would leave its mark. The way I finally got Algonquin 9618 fixed in my mind, where it still stands as staunchly and as uselessly as an iron hitching post in a concrete walk, was to bring in the World War. I saw that by subtracting 4 from the last two digits—18 —and adding it to the first two—96—I could make an even 100 of the first two. This made 14 out of the last two. I now had 10014 as a key number. This was useless unless I could plant in my memory some story, some war anecdote, which would break 10014 down into the proper arrangement of digits. The story I invented was this: that I had ended the war—that is, made '18 out of '14—by sending overseas a male quartet from my company of 100 men (I figured myself as captain of a company with the full regulation Civil War strength of 100 men). This gave me, logically and smoothly, 9618.

My invention of the war anecdote was the beginning of an elaborate system of remembering telephone numbers in which sometimes as many as seven wars were involved, together with the movement of not only male quartets but bowling teams, football squads, rowing crews, and the like. For instance, to remember one number, I figured myself as an officer in the war with Mexico (a certain Lieutenant Chelsea) who sent a baseball nine to the aid of Napoleon at the Battle of Waterloo. The key number was 4615; the correct reading 3724. I simply sent my 9 from '46 to '15, you see.

The danger of this kind of preoccupation lies in the likelihood of confusing fact with fancy, shadow with substance, one's imaginary character with one's actual character. My reactions and reflexes in the workaday world began to be prompted now and then by the nature of my responsibilities as an officer in wars that ended long ago. I would sometimes, in the office, bark commands at my superiors. Things finally got so bad that for more than two years I never phoned anybody. In this way I managed to slough off from my overburdened subconscious something in the neighborhood of a hundred and eighty numbers. Along with these vanished a lot of wearisome maneuvers, such as the activities of a golfing foursome in the Seminole Indian War, and the extraordinary advent of three basketball teams at the Battle of Saratoga. Now I am back to a fairly normal basis, with the phone numbers of only about ninety-five people thundering in the indexes of my mind. Of these people, I am in actual contact with perhaps thirty. The others have moved away, or have broken up housekeeping, or have cut me off, or are dead. Their silly phone numbers, however, linger still, often in the night marching wearily along the border of a dream, on their way back from Moscow, General Pierre Gustave Toutant Beauregard riding ahead, the American Davis Cup team of 1919 bringing up the rear. Hooting and mocking, laughing and crying, they pass in review, all the old, lost numbers.

I wish I were a member of Rudy Vallée's band, peacefully reading a detective story.

XIX. Back to the Grades

When I read in the newspapers that young James Cox Brady, who is a director in fifty corporations, had started shovelling coal in the boiler-room of one of them in order to learn the business, I was reminded of the time that I went back to grammar school. I reëntered the fifth grade, because it was in the fifth grade that I had first begun to lose my way; and also because the desks in the lower grades were too small for me—I couldn't get my knees under them. I feel that there is more to be learned by going back to the fifth grade than by shovelling coal in a boiler-room. All you can learn in the latter case is how to shovel coal into a boiler, which can't be much of a help to a director of a corporation. Young Mr. Brady may, of course, have had some idea of studying the psychology of his fellow-workers, but he is bound to be disappointed in that, because all boiler-workers are Slavs and all they ever say is "Strook 'em." Let us imagine Mr. Brady trying to get at the psychology of one of his shovel-mates, a Slav named Wieneszciewcz. "How do you like this life?" says Mr. Brady, between shovels. "Strook 'em," says Mr. Wieneszciewcz. "What do you do for relaxation and entertainment—after work hours, I mean?" asks Mr. Brady. "Strook 'em," says Mr. Wieneszciewcz. In a little under an hour, a director of a corporation is going to learn all there is to know about shovelling coal and what his fellow-workers are thinking. Going back to the fifth grade is a richer experience.

I was thirty-four going on thirty-five when I returned to grammar school. My failure to grasp sentence-parsing, fractions, decimals, long division, and, especially, "problems," had after a quarter of a century begun to show up in my life and work. Although a family man of property, I discovered that I didn't understand taxation, gas-meter readings, endowment or straight-pay insurance policies, compound or simple interest, time-tables, bank balances, and electric-light bills. Nor could I get much meaning out of the books and articles which were being written all the time on economics and politics. Long stretches of Walter Lippmann meant nothing to me. One evening after we had returned from a contract-bridge game, my wife said to me, earnestly: "You ought to go back to the fifth grade." I suggested just as earnestly that she, too, should start over again, beginning with the first grade (she is younger than I am), but we finally compromised on my going back to the fifth grade.

I went to live with my parents when I returned to the grammar grades. The first morning of school, I couldn't find my hat. "If you'd hang up your hat, you'd know where it was," my mother said. "Let him find it himself; don't you hunt for it," said my father. I finally found it in the dog house with my baseball glove. Miss Malloy (the same teacher I had had in the fifth grade in 1905) made me stay after school for being tardy. She didn't remember me at first, but she finally did. "My, you have shot up like a weed!" she said. I was somewhat embarrassed. "You have shot up like a weed, too," I said.

Since I was used to staying up until one and two o'clock in the morning, I never got to sleep at ten and was usually late for school. I had to stay after class and write, a hundred times, the lines beginning: "Lost, somewhere between sunrise and sunset, two golden hours." "Don't cramp your fingers; get a free and easy wrist motion," Miss Malloy said. "Aw," I said, and grinned. She told me to wipe the smile off my face. I wouldn't, and she made me learn "To a Water Fowl" by heart.

Long division came a trifle easier to me at thirty-four than it had when I was ten, but I was so bad at problems that I had to stay after class and clean the blackboard-erasers. It was fun leaning out the window and slapping them against the wall of the building; the chalk spurted like smoke from a gun and got into your nose, and the erasers left little white rectangles on the bricks. Afterward I drew a picture of Miss Malloy on the blackboard and went home.

Miss Malloy would stay after class and help me with my problems in arithmetic. I had brought her some applejack one morning and she would sip the applejack while I struggled with the problems. "I'll ask my father to help me with the problems," I said one afternoon when, at the end of an hour, I hadn't got anywhere and neither had Miss Malloy—except with the applejack. Miss Malloy didn't say anything. She looked at me. "Fines' atha ev' had," she said. "Fines' probblums ev' solve, too." She began to cry and I went home.

I started Father off on a problem about if twenty men can excavate two hundred and thirty cubic yards of earth in five and a half hours, how many cubic yards of earth can five men excavate in an hour and a quarter? Father had first failed to make anything of that problem about the time that the Wright brothers got their improbable airship off the ground at Kitty

Hawk, but he started in on it again with considerable assurance. His first answer came out in hours instead of yards; his next answer was 1,987,000 cubic yards, which he had arrived at by changing the hours into seconds; and he finally wound up by discovering what a fifth of a man could excavate in three months. "Men don't work on an hour-and-a-quarter schedule in practical experience," said Father, at last. Mother said that that wasn't the idea. "Then what *is* the idea?" shouted Father. The argument that followed aroused Grandfather, who for several years now had been laboring under the delusion that time had turned backward and that Father was courting Mother again. "Lovers' quarrels!" he cackled from the head of the stairs, and went cackling back to bed. He thought McKinley was President. I often wonder who he thought I was.

The next morning I told Mother I was too sick to go to school. "Where are you sick?" she said. I told her I had terrible pains in my stomach. "Be a big middle-aged soldier and get up!" she coaxed. "I don't want to be a big middle-aged soldier," I whined. She made me take some awful medicine. At breakfast, Father said he was going to take me out of school, that he and myself and Grandfather were simply losing ground all the time. He said he had dreamed about Christy Mathewson and the San Francisco earthquake and a lot of other things of twenty-five years ago. Grandfather said that Hayes had stolen the election from Tilden and to mark his words there would be hell to pay. Father told me I could go to school that day, for the last time, and get my books. "I don't propose to go through the fifth grade again at my age!" said Father, vehemently. Grandfather was furious. "You git your chores done and hike on to school or I'll whup your hide off!" he shouted at Father. We had to change the subject.

I didn't really drop out of school that day; I was thrown out. A little girl named Virginia Morrison, who sat at a desk across the aisle from me, had all the answers to the problems right. She was always laughing at me and sticking her tongue out at me from behind her geography. I finally pulled her hair, and she yelled. Miss Malloy came down the aisle and hit me across the hand with a ruler. I took the ruler away from her, sat on top of my desk, turned her over my knee, and spanked her.

My analyst (who is also losing ground steadily) told me later that it was a happy thing that I had been able to go back to school and spank my teacher. He said that noticeably good results would begin to show up in my life. They haven't, though.

XX. Hell Only Breaks Loose Once

(Written After Reading James M. Cain's "The Postman Always Rings Twice")

I

THEY kicked me out of college when I was about twenty-seven. I went up to see the Dean and tried to hand him a couple of laughs but it was no good. He said he couldn't put me back in college but I could hang around the office and sweep out and wash windows. I figured I better be rambling and I said I had a couple of other offers. He told me to sit down and think it over so I sat down.

Then she came in the room. She was tall and thin and had a white frowning forehead and soft eyes. She wasn't much to look at but she was something to think about. As far as she and I were concerned he wasn't in the room. She leaned over the chair where I was sitting and bit me in the ear. I let her have it right under the heart. It was a good one. It was plenty. She hit the floor like a two-year-old.

"What fell?" asked the Dean, peering over his glasses. I told him nothing fell.

II

After a while I said I guessed I'd hang around and go to work for him. "Do what?" he asked. He had forgot all about me, but I hung around. I liked him and he liked me but neither one of us cared what happened to the other.

When the Dean went out to lunch I walked into a rear office and she was there. I began to tremble all over like a hooch dancer. She was fussing with some papers but I could see she wasn't really doing anything. I walked close to her. It was like dying and going to Heaven. She was a little like my mother and a little like the time I got my hip busted in a football scrimmage. I reached over and let her have one on the chin and she went down like a tray of dishes. I knew then I would be beating her up the rest of my life. It made me feel like it was April and I was a kid again and had got up on a warm morning and it was all misty outdoors and the birds were singing.

III

"Hi, Dean," I said to him when he got back from lunch.

"What is it?" he asked. I could tell he thought he had never seen me before. I told him what it was. "Excellent," he said, looking surprised. He still didn't know what it was. She came out of the back room and he asked her what she wanted. He never remembered seeing anybody.

I took her out to lunch. It was sweet in the lunchroom and I kicked her under the table and broke her ankle. It was still broken when I carried her back to the Dean's office.

"Who do you wish to see?" he asked, looking over his glasses at us. I wanted to grind his glasses into his skull. She said we both worked there. He said that was excellent, but he wasn't looking for work. I told him to think it over and she and I went into the back room. I let her have one over the eye but it was a glancing blow and didn't knock her out. She cracked down on

me with a paperweight and I went out like a light but I took
her with me. She broke her head in the fall. We were uncon-
scious for about an hour. A couple of guys were bending over
us when we came to. They said they were from a place named
Lang's, a cleaning establishment. The Dean had got the idea we
were a bear rug and was going to send us out to be dry-cleaned.
He was pretty dumb but I liked him.

IV

"What do you want to work for that guy for?"
"I'm his secretary."
"What do you want to work for him for?"
"I said I'm his secretary."
"Keep talking."
"I have to work for him. He's my husband." I felt pretty sick
then.
"That's tough. You oughtn't to be married to him. He doesn't
know what it's all about."
"He lectures in his sleep."
"That must be swell."
"I don't want to be his wife. I want to be yours."
"You are mine."
"Let me have it again," she said. I gave her a short left jab
on the button. She was dizzy for days.

V

The Dean was too absent-minded to notice she was bruised
all the time. It made me sick seeing him sitting at his desk trying
to remember what it was all about. One day he began dictating
a letter to me but I didn't pay any attention. I went on dusting
a chair. Pretty soon he went out to lunch and I went in the back
room. She was there and I began to shiver like a tuning fork.
I stroked her hair. I had never done that before. It was like
going to sleep.

"There is one out for us," she told me.

"Okay," I said.

VI

He was sitting at his desk trying to figure out who he was when I hit him over the conk with an auto crank. I thought he would fold up like a leather belt, but he didn't. It didn't faze him. "Somebody's at the door," he said. I was shaking a little but I went to the door and opened it. There wasn't anybody there. I stood to one side so he could look out of the door into the hall. It was empty. "I thought I heard somebody knock," he said. It made me cold.

VII

We fixed him finally. I got him up on top of the university water tower one night to see the aurora borealis. There wasn't any aurora borealis but he was too dumb to notice that. It was swell up there on the tower. It smelled pretty. It smelled of jasmine. I felt like the first time I ever kissed a girl.

I rigged up one of those double flights of steps like tap-dancers dance up and down on and told him to get up on top of it.

"I don't want to get up on top of that," he said.

"You want to see the aurora borealis, don't you?"

"Most certainly."

"Then get up on top of that."

He got up on top of it and I climbed up after him. The thing was rickety but he didn't notice.

"What are we doing up here?" he asked me.

"Look at the aurora," I said, pointing at the sky. He looked and while we were standing there she came up on top of the steps with us. He didn't pay any attention to her. I swayed from side to side and started the thing teetering. I beat her up a little and then I beat him up a little. He looked like he had been spanked by an old aunt. The thing was swinging bad now, from one side to the other. I knew it was going over.

VIII

We all fell six flights. He was dead when they picked him up. She was dead too. I was near to her, but she was a long way off. I was dying, they told me. So I dictated this to a guy from the D.A.'s office, and here it is. And that's all, except I hope it's pretty in Heaven and smells like when the lilacs first come out on May nights in the Parc Monceau in Paris.

XXI. The Man Who Was Wetly

(After Reading an Anthology of British Short Stories)

A HALF-DOZEN of us were discussing that curious thing called life and the singular interrelationship between penalty and reward one night in the fireplace of the Cathay Cyclists' Club. "It seems rather warm in here, you know," said Empringham, who had, I knew, been wounded four times at Vimy Ridge. We moved out of the fireplace into the club room. It became a little cooler. Masters brought in another large tray of gooseberry wine and spiced walnuts, and for a time we were silent.

"Sitting in that fireplace," mused Empringham, finally, "reminded me of a curious adventure I had one night in New York City."

Lord Burleigh laughed. "I had supposed," he said, "that there were no singular adventures to be had in New York City. How about it, Buell?" This last was addressed to me, as being the only American present.

"Oh," I said, "we don't, of course, have your mysterious fog which shrouds London in a—ah——"

"Mysterious fog," put in little Bailey.

"Precisely," mused Empringham. "But I assure you there is mystery also to be found in clear streets. Shall I tell you my story?"

"No," said the Earl of Leaves, a bald, choleric man, who got up and abruptly left the room.

"Curious chap, Leaves," mused young Priestley. "I remember one night in the Sudan. A curious rain had come up and cooled that furnace of a jungle, in which you could hear Snider rifles squibbing wetly. Several of us subalterns were sitting around in our fatigue uniforms, when out of the jungle——"

"Jungle!" cried Empringham, slapping his leg. "The jungle is a state of mind. Your rain, my dear fellow, was a state of mind, too. Would it surprise you if I said that New York is also a jungle, also a state of mind?"

No one spoke for a minute.

"Let's see, where was I?" began young Priestley, again. "Oh, yes. It had rained, as I say, and the Sniders were squibbing——"

"Wetly," I prompted him, for Priestley had been wounded at Nantes and sometimes remembered rather slowly.

"Dear old Wetly!" cried Empringham. "What a chap he was! I last saw him in Port Said. God, how he had changed! At first I didn't know him. I was pricing some sherids at a native sampan in the marketplace when a fellow seized my shoulder—there in that hustings, that shambles! I supposed, of course, the man was a beggar and I threw off his arm a bit gruffly. 'Have on with you,' I said. 'Cheero, Empringham,' he said, and I saw that it was Wetly."

"That, of course," chimed in Leaves, who had returned to the room because he hadn't been able to find anything to do in any of the other rooms, "that is a decision which, at some time or other, in the lives of all of us, a man must make for

himself, all alone—without the help of God or man. Lord, what solitude can encompass a man in the midst of a teeming city!" He held up a curious object for us to look at. It did not seem, at first glance, extraordinary, being only a singular china figurine of a Napoleonic cavalryman standing beside his horse.

"Who is it?" asked Dunleavy, sourly. "Wetly?" We all fell silent, for it was unusual indeed when Kerry Dunleavy said anything. This was, in point of fact, the first thing he had said since 1908 when, fresh from Indian service, with the insignia of a subaltern on his shoulders, a pretty wife whom he had married God knows where, and the livid scar of a Sikh tamarinth across one cheek, he walked into the Cyclists' Club, took his old familiar chair, the leather one by the window, and called for a Scotch and soda.

"Damme," mused Dunleavy, "it was amazing, I tell you. There hadn't been a sound, except the drip, drip of rain falling from the huge leaves of the pelango trees, which the natives thatch their huts with. I was running over the company accounts at a little table, doing the best I could by the light of a beastly kerosene lamp and smoking that vile native tobacco to fend off the mosquitoes and flet-flet flies, when the door opened and a man wearing the uniform of Her Majesty's Death's Head Hussars staggered into the room. He was ghastly pale and, I could see at a glance, badly wounded at Ypres. Without a word he walked in an uncertain line over to the table and snatched up the champagne glass out of which I had been drinking that fiendish native pongo-pongo, or gluelike liqueur. He stood there wavering, then proposed a toast and——"

"Shattered the glass in his hand!" cried young Priestley.

"Good God!" cried Empringham, pushing back his chair and rising to his feet. We all stared at him.

"Take it easy, old chap," I said, for I liked Empringham and knew that his old wounds still bothered him.

"I say, what is the matter?" cried young Priestley, who was, as we all knew, too young to know what was the matter.

"Did he give this toast when he shattered that glass?" demanded Empringham, in an odd, strained voice, white as a sheet. "Did he say, when he broke that glass: 'The Queen, God bless her'?" There was a singular, strained silence. We all looked at Dunleavy.

"That," said Dunleavy in a low, tense voice, "that is what he said." Empringham fixed us all in turn with a curious, wide-eyed stare. Outside the rain beat against the windows. Empringham's chair toppled to the floor with a clatter as loud as that of a brass shield falling.

"Gentlemen," said Empringham, "that toast has not been drunk for more than one hundred and fifty years."

"Good God!" cried young Priestley.

"Good God!" muttered little Bailey.

"Good God!" I mused, softly. Old Masters moved over and took up the tray, its wine and walnuts untouched. He was about to turn away when, as if on second thought, he removed the walnut bowl and set it before us.

"Nuts, gentlemen," said Masters, and withdrew.

XXII. If Grant Had Been Drinking at Appomattox

(*Scribner's Magazine* published a series of three articles: "If Booth Had Missed Lincoln," "If Lee Had Not Won The Battle of Gettysburg," and "If Napoleon Had Escaped to America." This is the fourth.)

THE morning of the ninth of April, 1865, dawned beautifully. General Meade was up with the first streaks of crimson in the eastern sky. General Hooker and General Burnside were up, and had breakfasted, by a quarter after eight. The day continued beautiful. It drew on toward eleven o'clock. General Ulysses S. Grant was still not up. He was asleep in his famous old navy hammock, swung high above the floor of his headquarters' bedroom. Headquarters was distressingly disarranged: papers were strewn on the floor; confidential notes from spies scurried here and there in the breeze from an open window; the dregs of an overturned bottle of wine flowed pinkly across an important military map.

Corporal Shultz, of the Sixty-fifth Ohio Volunteer Infantry, aide to General Grant, came into the outer room, looked around him, and sighed. He entered the bedroom and shook the General's hammock roughly. General Ulysses S. Grant opened one eye.

"Pardon, sir," said Corporal Shultz, "but this is the day of surrender. You ought to be up, sir."

"Don't swing me," said Grant, sharply, for his aide was making the hammock sway gently. "I feel terrible," he added, and he turned over and closed his eye again.

"General Lee will be here any minute now," said the Corporal firmly, swinging the hammock again.

"Will you cut that out?" roared Grant. "D'ya want to make me sick, or what?" Shultz clicked his heels and saluted. "What's he coming here for?" asked the General.

"This is the day of surrender, sir," said Shultz. Grant grunted bitterly.

"Three hundred and fifty generals in the Northern armies," said Grant, "and he has to come to *me* about this. What time is it?"

"You're the Commander-in-Chief, that's why," said Corporal Shultz. "It's eleven twenty-five, sir."

"Don't be crazy," said Grant. "Lincoln is the Commander-in-Chief. Nobody in the history of the world ever surrendered before lunch. Doesn't he know that an army surrenders on its stomach?" He pulled a blanket up over his head and settled himself again.

"The generals of the Confederacy will be here any minute now," said the Corporal. "You really ought to be up, sir."

Grant stretched his arms above his head and yawned.

"All right, all right," he said. He rose to a sitting position and stared about the room. "This place looks awful," he growled.

"You must have had quite a time of it last night, sir," ventured Shultz.

"Yeh," said General Grant, looking around for his clothes. "I was wrassling some general. Some general with a beard."

Shultz helped the commander of the Northern armies in the field to find his clothes.

"Where's my other sock?" demanded Grant. Shultz began to look around for it. The General walked uncertainly to a table and poured a drink from a bottle.

"I don't think it wise to drink, sir," said Shultz.

"Nev' mind about me," said Grant, helping himself to a second, "I can take it or let it alone. Didn' ya ever hear the story about the fella went to Lincoln to complain about me drinking too much? 'So-and-So says Grant drinks too much,' this fella said. 'So-and-So is a fool,' said Lincoln. So this fella went to What's-His-Name and told him what Lincoln said and he came roarin' to Lincoln about it. 'Did you tell So-and-So I was a fool?' he said. 'No,' said Lincoln, 'I thought he knew it.'" The General smiled, reminiscently, and had another drink. "*That's* how I stand with Lincoln," he said, proudly.

The soft thudding sound of horses' hooves came through the open window. Shultz hurriedly walked over and looked out.

"Hoof steps," said Grant, with a curious chortle.

"It is General Lee and his staff," said Shultz.

"Show him in," said the General, taking another drink. "And see what the boys in the back room will have."

Shultz walked smartly over to the door, opened it, saluted, and stood aside. General Lee, dignified against the blue of the April sky, magnificent in his dress uniform, stood for a moment framed in the doorway. He walked in, followed by his staff. They bowed, and stood silent. General Grant stared at them. He only had one boot on and his jacket was unbuttoned.

"I know who you are," said Grant. "You're Robert Browning, the poet."

"This is General Robert E. Lee," said one of his staff, coldly.

"Oh," said Grant. "I thought he was Robert Browning. He certainly looks like Robert Browning. There was a poet for you, Lee: Browning. Did ja ever read 'How They Brought the Good News from Ghent to Aix'? 'Up Derek, to saddle, up

Derek, away; up Dunder, up Blitzen, up Prancer, up Dancer, up Bouncer, up Vixen, up——'"

"Shall we proceed at once to the matter in hand?" asked General Lee, his eyes disdainfully taking in the disordered room.

"Some of the boys was wrassling here last night," explained Grant. "I threw Sherman, or some general a whole lot like Sherman. It was pretty dark." He handed a bottle of Scotch to the commanding officer of the Southern armies, who stood holding it, in amazement and discomfiture. "Get a glass, somebody," said Grant, looking straight at General Longstreet. "Didn't I meet you at Cold Harbor?" he asked. General Longstreet did not answer.

"I should like to have this over with as soon as possible," said Lee. Grant looked vaguely at Shultz, who walked up close to him, frowning.

"The surrender, sir, the surrender," said Corporal Shultz in a whisper.

"Oh sure, sure," said Grant. He took another drink. "All right," he said. "Here we go." Slowly, sadly, he unbuckled his sword. Then he handed it to the astonished Lee. "There you are, General," said Grant. "We dam' near licked you. If I'd been feeling better we *would* of licked you."

XXIII. One More April

(An Effort to Start Another Novel about the Galsworthy Characters, Taking Them Up Where He Left Off)

On the second day after the sailing of the transatlantic liner *Picardy* for America, in April, 1935, three English people who were unknown to each other came into the main dining saloon from wholly different staterooms and began to play piquet together. This breach of form affected them all in precisely the same way: each one sat perhaps seven feet from the card table so that, even with arms extended at full length, it was impossible to bring the cards near enough to the playing surface to lay them upon it. One of these three was a young woman of about twenty-two, one a darkish man of perhaps forty-three, and one a man of between ninety-five and a hundred.

The younger man spoke suddenly.

The effect of his breach of form on the others was diverse: the olderish man leaned forward as if to examine the table legs, with a sort of weathered skepticism; the young woman turned a surprised look upon the speaker.

"Didn't I meet you at my wedding?" she queried. "I am

Fleur Desert, the second daughter of Dinny Mont, who married Wilfrid Desert; the first daughter was Celia. There are two brothers, Michael and Michael." The younger man's mouth lost its disdainful look.

"I am your sister's brother-in-law, Cherrill Desert."

The older man spoke unexpectedly.

"Forsyte Desert's nephew, eh? Old Derek Mont's cousin. What's become of young Cherrill Desert? Still wandering sallowly about the East, I'll wager, writing verse."

Desert smiled and shook his head.

"I am Cherrill Desert," he said. The older man looked surprised.

"And probably died there," he grunted.

Fleur Desert thought: "He can't have been home for many years."

"Cherrill Desert married Dinny Mont's second daughter, Fleur," she said. "They have two children, Dinny and Fleur." A slight colour stained her cheeks. The disdainful look which had been about to return to the young man's lips did not.

"I remember you perfectly," he said. "You are Wilfrid Desert's daughter."

"Old Derek Mont's cousin's wife," said the older man, with

a sort of skeptical weatheredness. "Forsyte Desert's niece-in-law."

The other two looked at him with frank surprise.

"I am Uncle Adrian," said the older man. "Or his brother, Mark. I cannot always remember which. However, if I'm Mark, he's going to be confoundedly seasick." He glared about the saloon, which was filled with surprised card tables. "I like the way these tables stand up," he said. The ship rocked a bit. "Mark never had a stomach for the ocean." He chuckled unexpectedly.

Fleur thought: "He's Adrian. Uncle Lawrence always said Adrian Mont knew tables."

The older man gave up his study of the card tables.

"Rather leggish. But they hold up." He took out a surprised old watch which chimed the days and months and years. It struck April fifth, 1935.

"My goodness! Aunt Sheila's birthday!" cried Fleur. "And I've forgotten to send her a radiogram!"

The older man smiled and spoke abruptly.

"I was at Somebody Mont's, or her mother's," he said, "the day that all these birthday parties started. Ronald Ferse was there, and a small Chinese boy, and Aunt Alison and her youngest, little Anne, and Uncle Hilary and Tony. Monty Muskham, too—who became Musky Montham. The war turned him around. And Uncle Lawrence, my father's brother. And the Dingo children, Celia and Moriston." He frowned. "All scattered now. All scattered then, as far as that goes."

The disdainful look returned to the younger man's lips.

"Ronald Ferse is in coal and feed, Hilary and Tony's daughter, Jean, went in for one-old-cat behind Government House in Rangoon. I don't know what became of the Chinese boy. Uncle Lawrence is translating the Foreign Office records into Russian for the Soviet—confounded officialism! The Dingo children married each other and broke old Forsyte Dingo's heart."

"Forsyte Dingo was in love with Celia Dingo, wasn't he?" queried the more weathered of the two men. The dark look deepened on the face of the more disdainful of the two men.

"Forsyte Dingo was her father," he said. "And her father-in-law, too—after she married her brother."

The old man chuckled unexpectedly.

"Like to see old Forsyte again," he said. "The two of us could play four-handed bridge." He looked at Dinny Mont's daughter, for whose mother he had gone away to the East. He wondered who she was. It didn't make much difference. All these women, he understood, were the same woman; he was two men, like old Forsyte Dingo, and outnumbered them all. Perhaps it was what kept him going—that and his nice eye for tables—providing he was Adrian. Mark Mont was never a man for tables. The old man twiddled the setting arrangement of his watch, turning it back to 1894, and suddenly discovered that, except for his shoes and socks, his legs were quite bare. Through some surprising and unexpected oversight he had forgotten to put on his trousers. This breach of form had an immediate effect on the others. Wilfrid Desert's son-in-law arose and so did Dinny Mont's daughter. The older man's face was masked in a sort of shrewd suspicion.

"I for one," he said, "shall never leave this spot." The young man laughed and turned his dark eyes on Fleur.

"Will you have lunch with me tomorrow?" he queried.

"I will. Where?"

"Right here on the ship. It'll be easier. We're two days out, you know." They crossed the saloon together.

Fleur thought: "He's as quick as ever. He sees through things."

The older man sat where he was—where, indeed, he intended always to sit unless they came and carried him away, or brought him the rest of his clothes. "England, England!" he murmured. It disturbed him that Adrian Mont, the solid one of the two Mont brothers, should lose his pants. Suddenly he began to feel sickish.

With a faint smile of relief, he thought: "I'm Mark!"

XXIV. How to See a Bad Play

ONE of my friends, who is a critic of the drama, invited me to accompany him last season to all the plays which he suspected were not going to be good enough or interesting enough to take his girl to. His suspicions were right in each instance, and there were dozens of instances. I don't know why I kept accepting his invitations to first nights of dubious promise, but I did. Perhaps it was sheer fascination. I know a man, an inveterate smoker of five-cent cigars, who once refused my offer of a Corona: he said he just couldn't go the things. Bad plays can get that kind of hold on you; anyway, they did on me. (I'm not going to go to *any* plays this season; I'm going to ski, and play lotto.)

I still brood about some of the situations, characters, tactics, and strategies I ran into last season in the more awful plays. I thank whatever gods may be that very few lines of dialogue, however, come back at night to roost above my chamber door. As a matter of fact, the only line that haunts me is one from

"Reprise," during the first scene of the first act of which a desperate young man is prevented from jumping off the balustrade of a penthouse (all plays set in penthouses are terrible) by another young man. The desperate young man then has three or four shots of what he describes as "excellent brandy" and the other man asks him if he still wants to jump. "No," says the desperate young man. "Your brandy has taken my courage." That marked the first time in the history of the world when three or four slugs of excellent brandy took a desperate man's courage. I find myself thinking about it.

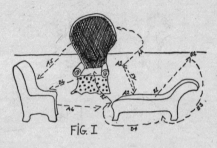

FIG. I

It was in this very same play, "Reprise" (or was it "Yesterday's Orchids"?), that the double-wing-back formation and triple lateral pass reached a new height. I have drawn a little diagram (Fig. 1) to illustrate what I mean. There was really no business in the play, only a great deal of talk, and the director must have found out early—probably during the first rehearsal—that the way the play was written the characters were just going to sit in chairs or on chaise longues and talk to each other, so he got them to moving around. After all, there has to be action of some kind in every play. Fig. 1 shows one of the more intricate moves that were made, as accurately as I can remember it now (I may have left out a couple of shifts, but it's close enough). Character A, to begin with, is standing at the right (A 1) of the handsome chair, centre rear, and Character B is sitting (B 1) on the chaise longue. A moves over (A 2) and sits on the foot of the chaise longue, whereupon B gets up and moves to position B 2 and then around the chaise longue (B 3) to the same place he had been sitting, as A reverses his field (A 3), circles around the big chair (A 4), and goes to the little chair (A 5). B now moves to the foot of the chaise longue (B 4), and then goes over and sits in the big chair (B 5). As he does so, A moves over and sits on the foot of the chaise longue again (A 6), then B crosses to the little

FIG. 2

chair (B 6), thus completing a full circle, with variations. All this time a lot of dialogue was going on, dealing with some brand-new angle on sex, but I was so engrossed in following the maze of crisscrosses that I didn't take in any of it, and hence, as far as sex knowledge goes, I am just where I was before I went to the play. There were a great many other involved crossings and recrossings, and what are known on the gridiron as Statue of Liberty plays, in this drama, but the one I have presented here was my favorite.

Another formation that interested me in several of the plays I studied was what I call the back-to-back emotional scene (Fig. 2). The two characters depicted here are, strange as it

may seem, "talking it out." In some plays in which this formation occurred they were declaring their love for each other; in
others she was telling him that she was in love with someone
else, or he was telling her that he had to go to South America
because he was in love with her sister or because he thought
she was in love with his brother, or his father-in-law, or something of the sort. I have witnessed a number of emotional
scenes in real life, but I have just happened to miss any in

which the parties involved moved past each other and faced
things out back to back. Apparently I don't get around as
much as playwrights do.

Fig. 3 illustrates another position that was frequently to be
seen on our stage last season: the woman, standing, comforting
the man, sitting. In this curious entanglement, so different
from anything that has ever happened to me, the position of
the arms is always just as I have shown it in the picture and
the woman's head is always lifted, as if she were studying a
cobweb in a far corner of the ceiling. Sometimes she closes her
eyes, whereupon the man opens his. When they break away,
it is quite simple to go into the back-to-back formation. Some
years ago, along about the time of "Merton of the Movies," the
comforting scene was done in quite a different manner: the

woman sat on the chair, and the man got down on his knees and put his head in her lap. But times have changed.

In Fig. 4, we take up the character who bobbed up (and down) oftenest in last year's bad plays (she bobbed up and down in some of the better plays, too, but mostly in the bad plays); namely, the elderly lady who is a good sport, a hard drinker, and an authority on sex. There was one such lady in the forgettable "Yesterday's Reprise" (or was it "Orchids"?). She could get away with half a quart of brandy between dinner time and bedtime (3 A.M.), and when she went to bed finally

FIG. 4.

she took the bottle with her—"I'm going to put a nipple on this thing and go to bed," she announced as she made her exit. This type of old lady was also given to a stream of epigrams, such as: "At twenty, one is in love with love; at thirty, love is in love with one; at forty, one is in love with two; at fifty, one does not care what two are in love with one; and at sixty," etc., etc. It doesn't have to make a great deal of sense; the sophisticates in the audience always laugh, and one or two who have been through a lot applaud.

There were a lot of other trick moves, positions, and characters in last year's plays, but I have neither the time nor the inclination to remind you of all of them. In winding up the season, I might mention two postures that were very prevalent. It was customary, in the theatre of 1934-35, for juveniles to sit down backward, or wrong-side-out, in straight chairs—that is, facing the back of the chair with their arms crossed on the top of it and their chins on their arms. This position indicated nonchalance and restless energy. Of course, it has been resorted to for years (and years), but last season was the biggest season for it that I can recall; almost no man under forty-five sat down with his back to the chair back. Another popular position—for juveniles and ingénues—was sitting on the extreme edge of a davenport or chaise longue. It seems that nowadays a young couple in love never relax and lean back against anything; they must sit (and it is one of the few face-to-face postures in the modern theatre) on the very edge of whatever they are sitting on, their legs thrust backward, their bodies inclined sharply forward, their eyes sparkling, and their words coming very fast. From this position, as from the standing-sitting position (Fig. 3), it is easy to stand up, work the double-crossing maneuver, and go into the back-to-back emotional scene. Apparently young people no longer meet on their feet, face to face, and engage in the obsolete practice of putting their arms around each other. As I say, times have changed. Or maybe it's only the theatre that has changed.

XXV. How to Listen to a Play

PRACTICALLY all the people I know who write plays want to read them to me. Furthermore, they do read them to me. I don't know why they select me to read plays to, because I am a very bad listener indeed, one of the worst listeners in the United States. I am always waiting for people to stop talking, or reading plays, so that I can talk, or read plays. Unfortunately, I have no plays to read to people (although I am always planning to write some) and, at forty, I do not talk as fast as I used to, or get into it as quickly, so that people with plays under their arms, or in their hip pockets, or even just vaguely outlined in their minds, get the jump on me. It is in the lobby of a hotel which I shall call the Cherokee that I am most often trapped by play readers. I frequently wander into the lobby looking for my hat or overcoat, which I am in the habit of forgetting and leaving there. Play readers seem to know this, for they are generally lurking near where I have left my hat or coat, waiting to pounce. They pounce very fast. "Listen!" a play reader will say, confronting me without even a hello or a how-are-you. "The action takes place in a roadside hot-dog stand, with the usual what's-its-names and so-and-sos scattered here and there, a gasoline pump down right, and a cabin or two on the backdrop. Ella is this girl in charge of the stand; she is pretty, charming, and intelligent but can't get away from the stand to go to school or anything on account of her paralyzed mother, who is paralyzed but sinister, and very strong—she's the menace, see, but she doesn't come on until later. Ella is arranging the salt and mustard and what's-this on the counter when Harry comes on. Ella: 'Hello, Harry.' Harry: 'Hello, Ella.' You can see they are in love——"

"Who can?" I used to ask, bitterly, or "How can you?", but I gave that up because interruptions other than "That's fine," "Swell," and the like are lost on people who read plays to you. What I usually do now is find a comfortable chair, lean back, close my eyes, put an index finger alongside one cheek, and, frowning slightly, pretend to be engrossed. It used to be difficult to do this for more than one act without dozing, but now I can do it for all three, saying "That's fine" or "Swell" at intervals, although I haven't actually taken in a word. A semi-doze, which even now I occasionally lapse into, is worse than complete sleep, because one finds oneself, in a semi-doze, now and then answering questions in the script. For instance, this question occurred in the second act of a play a woman was reading to me recently: "How've you been, Jim?" "Fine," I answered, coming out of my doze without quite knowing where I was. "How've *you* been?" That was a terrible moment for both of us, but I got out of it some way.

Some play readers buy you drinks while you listen, but you can't count on it, and it really isn't a good idea to drink during the reading of a three-act play, because it takes about an hour and a half to read a three-act play and you can get pretty cockeyed in an hour and a half, especially if you are keeping your mind a blank. Many a time I have walked unsteadily out of the Cherokee at three-thirty in the afternoon, drunk as a lord, with nothing left to do but go to my apartment and go to sleep. As a rule, on these occasions I wake up about ten-thirty P.M., having accomplished nothing and with the whole heavy dull night ahead of me. Play readers don't care about that. They are selfish people.

I can think of no plays, no matter how fine, from "Macbeth" to "What Price Glory?", that I would like to have read to me. I like to see them played or to read them myself, but I have never liked having *anything* read to me (the italics have been mine since I was a little boy). But no playwright will turn his play over to you (or at least he won't to me) so that it can be read alone and at your convenience. Playwrights like to read their plays aloud, because they think you will miss the full rich flavor of certain scenes if they don't. They do not seem to realize that a woman reading a man's part, or a man reading a woman's part, is not only dull but ineffective; but I do, I realize it.

Seven or eight years ago, when I first started in listening to plays, I would actually absorb the sense of the first few scenes before my mind began to wander and my eyes to rove. It really is advisable to comprehend a little of what has been read to you, because the moment is bound to come when the man or woman actually finishes the thing and stops reading. Then he or she is going to say, "Well, what do you think of the character of Rose?" The only thing to say to this is "I think the character of Rose is fine. You've got her down beautifully"; then you can go back quickly to the first scene of the first act (the one you listened to) and dwell on that. No playwright wants to dwell very long with you on the first scene of his first act (they are always crazy about their second and third acts), but if you are adroit enough, you can always work back to that first scene no matter what the playwright wants to have your opinion on. "That," you can say of the second or third act, "is perfect as it stands, perfect. I wouldn't change a line. Nor would I in that magnificent first scene where Ella and Harry discover they are in love." Etc., etc.

It is useless to rely on some friend, wandering around the lobby, to extricate you from your predicament. I've tried that and it only caused more anguish. Once, when a playwright was slowly nearing his second-act curtain (where Harry and Ella rediscover that they are in love, or discover that they are not in love, or are in love with someone else, as the play may be), I slyly signalled a friend to come to my rescue. He walked over to where the playwright and I were sitting. "Good Lord!" I cried, jumping to my feet and facing the newcomer. "I completely forgot about you! We're late now, aren't we? We'll have to hurry!" He stared at me. "Late for what? Hurry where?" he asked. I had a frightful time getting out of that.

If the play reader is bad, the plot outliner is even worse, because you don't have to meet the eyes of the reader, he being intent on his manuscript, but you can't get away from the eyes of the outliner He usually begins something like this: "There's this girl, see, and the guy, and her paralyzed mother, who she suspects knows where she has hidden the franchise and naturally doesn't want Ella to leave the room because he'll get it. She knows that Ella is in love with Ella—I mean Harry, the fellow, see?—but the old girl sees through him even if she doesn't, only she can't talk, she can't speak, see, and let the girl know, let Ella know her suspicions." Even if you listen with intense concentration, you can't follow the plot of a plot outliner. It gets more and more involved as it goes along and is bound to be filled with such terms as "upstage" and "downstage," which I always get mixed up so that I don't know where I am, or where Ella is or the old lady.

I am trying to be kind and considerate to everybody, out of

repentance for the life I have led, but some day a play reader or a plot outliner is going to push me too far and I am going to get up in the middle of the first scene and scream. I am going to scream until the manager comes. I am going to scream until the ambulance and the police and the photographers come. I don't care how much people may talk.

XXVI. The Funniest Man
You Ever Saw

EVERYBODY seemed surprised that I had never met Jack Klohman.

"Judas, I didn't know there was anybody who didn't know
Jack Klohman," said Mr. Potter, who was big and heavy, of
body and mind. "He's funnier'n hell." Mr. Potter laughed and
slapped his knee. "He's the funniest man you ever saw."

"He certainly is funny," said somebody else.

"He's marvellous," drawled a woman I didn't like. Looking
around the group I discovered I didn't like any of them much,
except Joe Mayer. This was undoubtedly unfair, for Joe was
the only one I knew very well. The others had come over to
the table where we were sitting. Somebody had mentioned Jack
Klohman and everybody had begun to laugh.

"Do you know him, Joe?" I asked.

"I know him," said Joe, without laughing.

"Judas," went on Potter, "I'll never forget one night at Jap
Rudolph's. Klohman was marvellous that night. This was a

couple years ago, when Ed Wynn was here in a new show—let's see, what the devil was it? Not 'The Crazy Fool.'"

"'The Perfect Fool,'" said somebody else.

"Yes. But it wasn't that," said Potter. "What the dickens was it? Well, never mind; anyway there was a scene in it where——"

"Was it 'Simple Simon'?" asked the blonde girl who was with Creel.

"No. It was a couple years before that," said Potter.

"Oh, I know," said the blonde girl. "It was—now wait—it was 'The Manhatters'!"

"Ed Wynn wasn't in that," said Creel. "Wynn wasn't in that show."

"Well, it doesn't make much difference," said Potter. "Anyway, in this scene he has a line where——"

"'Manhattan Mary'!" cried Griswold.

"That's it!" said Potter, slapping his knee. "Well, in this scene he comes on with a rope, kind of a lariat——"

"Halter," said Griswold. "It was a halter."

"Yes, that's right," said Potter. "Anyway, he comes on with this halter——"

"Who comes on?" asked Joe Mayer. "Klohman?"

"No, no," said Potter. "Wynn comes on with the halter and walks up to the footlights and some guy asks him what he's got the rope for, what he's doing with the halter. 'Well,' says Wynn, 'I've either lost a horse or found a piece of rope——'"

"I think he said: 'I've either found a piece of rope or lost a horse,'" said Griswold. "Losing the horse coming last is funnier."

"Well, anyway," said Potter, "Jack Klohman used to elaborate on the idea and this night at Jap Rudolph's I thought we'd all pass away."

"I nearly did," said Joe Mayer.

"What did this Klohman do?" I asked finally, cutting in on the general laughter.

"Well," said Potter, "he'd go out into the kitchen, see, and come in with a Uneeda biscuit and he'd say: 'Look, I've either lost a biscuit box or found a cracker'—that's the right order, Gris—'I've either lost a biscuit box or lost'—I mean found—'a cracker.'"

"I guess you're right," said Griswold.

"It sounds right," said Joe Mayer.

"Then he'd do the same thing with everything he picked up, no matter what," said Potter. "Finally he went out of the room and was gone half an hour or so and then he comes down the stairs and holds up this faucet and says: 'I've either lost a bathtub or found a faucet.' He'd unscrewed a faucet from the bathtub and comes downstairs with this faucet—see what I mean? Laugh? I thought I'd pass away."

Everybody who had been at Jap Rudolph's that night roared with laughter.

"But that wasn't anything," said Potter. "Wait'll you hear. Along about two in the morning he slips out again, see?—all the way out of the house this time. Well, I'll be doggoned if that guy didn't come back carrying part of an honest-to-God chancel rail! He did! I'm telling you! Son-of-a-gun had actually got into a church somehow and wrenched part of this chancel rail loose and there he was standing in the door and he says: 'I've either lost a church or found a chancel rail.' It was rich. It was the richest thing I ever saw. Helen Rudolph had gone to bed, I remember—she wasn't very well—but we got her up and he did it again. It was rich."

"Sounds like a swell guy to have around," I said.

"You'd darn near pass away," said Potter.

"You really would," said Joe Mayer.

"He's got a new gag now," said one of the women. "He's got a new gag that's as funny as the dickens. He keeps taking

things out of his pockets or off of a table or something and says that he's just invented them. He always takes something that's been invented for *years*, say like a lead pencil or something, and goes into this long story about how he thought it up one night. I remember he did it with about twenty different things one night at Jap's——"

"Jap Rudolph's?" I asked.

"Yes," said the woman. "He likes to drop in on them, so you can usually find him there, so we usually drop in on them too. Well, this night he took out a package of those Life Savers and handed us each one of the mints and——"

"Oh, yes, I remember that!" said Potter, slapping his knee and guffawing.

"Gave us each one of these mints," went on the woman, "and asked us what we thought of them—asked us whether we thought they'd go or not. 'It's a little thing I thought up one day,' he said. Then he'd go on with a long rigmarole about how he happened to think of the idea, and——"

"And then he'd take a pencil out of his pocket," cut in Potter, "and ask you what you thought of the eraser on the end of it. 'Just a little gadget I thought up the other night,' he'd say. Then he says he'll show you what it's for, so he makes everybody take a piece of paper and he says: 'Now everybody make some pencil marks on the paper; any kind—I won't look,' so then he goes into another room and says to let him know when you're ready. So we all make marks on the pieces of paper and somebody goes and gets him out of the other room——"

"They always go and get him out of the other room," Joe Mayer said to me.

"Sure," said Potter. "So he comes out with his sleeves rolled up, like a magician, and——"

"But the *funniest* thing he does," began the woman whom Potter had interrupted.

"And he gathers up the papers and erases the marks with

the eraser and he says: 'Oh, it's just a novelty; I'm not going to try to market it.' Laugh? I thought I'd pass away. Of course you really ought to see him do it; the way he does it is a big part of it—solemn and all; he's always solemn, always acts solemn about it."

"The *funniest* thing he does," began the interrupted woman again, loudly, "is fake card tricks. He——"

"Oh, yes!" cried Potter, roaring and slapping his knee. "He does these fake card tricks. He——" Here the recollection of the funny man's antics proved too much for Potter and he laughed until he cried. It was several minutes before he could control himself. "He'll take a pack of cards," he finally began again. "He'll take a pack of cards——" Once more the image of Klohman taking a pack of cards was too much for the narrator and he went off into further gales of laughter. "He'll take this pack of cards," Potter eventually said once more, wiping his eyes, "and ask you to take any card and you take one and then he says: 'Put it anywhere in the deck' and you do and then he makes a lot of passes and so on——"

"Like a magician," said Joe Mayer.

"Yes," said Potter. "And then he draws out the wrong card, or maybe he *looks* at your card first and then goes through the whole deck till he finds it and shows it to you or——"

"Sometimes he just lays the pack down and acts as if he'd never started any trick," said Griswold.

"Does he do imitations?" I asked. Joe Mayer kicked my shins under the table.

"Does he do *imitations*?" bellowed Potter. "Wait'll I tell you——"

XXVII. The Black Magic
of Barney Haller

It was one of those hot days on which the earth is uninhabitable; even as early as ten o'clock in the morning, even on the hill where I live under the dark maples. The long porch was hot and the wicker chair I sat in complained hotly. My coffee was beginning to wear off and with it the momentary illusion it gives that things are Right and life is Good. There were sultry mutterings of thunder. I had a quick feeling that if I looked up from my book I would see Barney Haller. I looked up, and there he was, coming along the road, lightning playing about his shoulders, thunder following him like a dog.

Barney is (or was) my hired man. He is strong and amiable, sweaty and dependable, slowly and heavily competent. But he is also eerie: he trafficks with the devil. His ears twitch when he talks, but it isn't so much that as the things he says. Once in late June, when all of a moment sabres began to flash brightly in the heavens and bowling balls rumbled, I took refuge in the barn. I always have a feeling that I am going to

) 159 (

be struck by lightning and either riven like an old apple tree or left with a foot that aches in rainy weather and a habit of fainting. Those things happen. Barney came in, not to escape the storm to which he is, or pretends to be, indifferent, but to put the scythe away. Suddenly he said the first of those things that made me, when I was with him, faintly creepy. He pointed at the house. "Once I see dis boat come down de rock," he said. It is phenomena like that of which I stand in constant dread: boats coming down rocks, people being teleported, statues dripping blood, old regrets and dreams in the form of Luna moths fluttering against the windows at midnight.

Of course I finally figured out what Barney meant—or what I comforted myself with believing he meant: something about a bolt coming down the lightning rod on the house; a commonplace, an utterly natural thing. I should have dismissed it, but it had its effect on me. Here was a stolid man, smelling of hay and leather, who talked like somebody out of Charles Fort's books, or like a traveller back from Oz. And all the time the lightning was zigging and zagging around him.

On this hot morning when I saw Barney coming along with his faithful storm trudging behind him, I went back frowningly to my copy of "Swann's Way." I hoped that Barney, seeing me absorbed in a book, would pass by without saying anything. I read: ". . . I myself seemed actually to have become the subject of my book: a church, a quartet, the rivalry between Francis I and Charles V . . ." I could feel Barney standing looking at me, but I didn't look at him.

"Dis morning bime by," said Barney, "I go hunt grotches in de voods."

"That's fine," I said, and turned a page and pretended to be engrossed in what I was reading. Barney walked on; he had wanted to talk some more, but he walked on. After a paragraph or two, his words began to come between me and the words in the book. "Bime by I go hunt grotches in de voods."

If you are susceptible to such things, it is not difficult to visualize grotches. They fluttered into my mind: ugly little creatures, about the size of whippoorwills, only covered with blood and honey and the scrapings of church bells. Grotches . . . Who and what, I wondered, really was this thing in the form of a' hired man that kept anointing me ominously, in passing, with abracadabra?

Barney didn't go toward the woods at once; he weeded the corn, he picked apple boughs up off the lawn, he knocked a yellow jacket's nest down out of a plum tree. It was raining now, but he didn't seem to notice it. He kept looking at me out of the corner of his eye, and I kept looking at him out of the corner of my eye. "Vot dime is it, blease?" he called to me finally. I put down my book and sauntered out to him. "When you go for those grotches," I said, firmly, "I'll go with you." I was sure he wouldn't want me to go. I was right; he protested that he could get the grotches himself. "I'll go with you," I said, stubbornly. We stood looking at each other. And then, abruptly, just to give *him* something to ponder over, I quoted:

> "I'm going out to clean the pasture spring;
> I'll only stop to rake the leaves away
> (And wait to watch the water clear, I may):
> I shan't be gone long.—You come too."

It wasn't, I realized, very good abracadabra, but it served: Barney looked at me in a puzzled way. "Yes," he said, vaguely.
"It's five minutes of twelve," I said, remembering he had asked.
"Den we go," he said, and we trudged through the rain over to the orchard fence and climbed that, and opened a gate and went out into the meadow that slopes up to the woods. I had a prefiguring of Barney, at some proper spot deep in the woods, prancing around like a goat, casting off his false nature, shed-

ding his hired man's garments, dropping his Teutonic accent, repeating diabolical phrases, conjuring up grotches.

There was a great slash of lightning and a long bumping of thunder as we reached the edge of the woods.

I turned and fled. Glancing over my shoulder, I saw Barney standing and staring after me. . . .

It turned out (on the face of it) to be as simple as the boat that came down the rock. Grotches were "crotches": crotched saplings which he cut down to use as supports under the peach boughs, because in bearing time they became so heavy with fruit that there was danger of the branches snapping off. I saw Barney later, putting the crotches in place. We didn't have much to say to each other. I can see now that he was beginning to suspect me too.

About six o'clock next evening, I was alone in the house and sleeping upstairs. Barney rapped on the door of the front porch. I knew it was Barney because he called to me. I woke up slowly. It was dark for six o'clock. I heard rumblings and saw flickerings. Barney was standing at the front door with his storm at heel! I had the conviction that it wasn't storming anywhere except around my house. There couldn't, without the intervention of the devil or one of his agents, be so many lightning storms in one neighborhood.

I had been dreaming of Proust and the church at Combray and *madeleines* dipped in tea, and the rivalry between Francis I and Charles V. My head whirled and I didn't get up. Barney kept on rapping. He called out again. There was a flash, followed by a sharp splitting sound. I leaped up. This time, I thought, he is here to get me. I had a notion that he was standing at the door barefooted, with a wreath of grape leaves around his head, and a wild animal's skin slung over his shoulder. I didn't want to go down, but I did.

) 162 (

He was as usual, solid, amiable, dressed like a hired man. I went out on the porch and looked at the improbable storm, now on in all its fury. "This is getting pretty bad," I said, meaningly. Barney looked at the rain placidly. "Well," I said, irritably, "what's up?" Barney turned his little squinty blue eyes on me.

"We go to the garrick now and become warbs," he said.

"The hell we do!" I thought to myself, quickly. I was uneasy —I was, you might even say, terrified—but I determined not to show it. If he began to chant incantations or to make obscene signs or if he attempted to sling me over his shoulder, I resolved to plunge right out into the storm, lightning and all, and run to the nearest house. I didn't know what they would think at the nearest house when I burst in upon them, or what I would tell them. But I didn't intend to accompany this amiable-looking fiend to any garrick and become a warb. I tried to persuade myself that there was some simple explanation, that warbs would turn out to be as innocuous as boats on rocks and grotches in the woods, but the conviction gripped me (in the growling of the thunder) that here at last was the Moment when Barney Haller, or whoever he was, had chosen to get me. I walked toward the steps that lead to the lawn, and turned and faced him, grimly.

"Listen!" I barked, suddenly. "Did you know that even when it isn't brillig I can produce slithy toves? Did you happen to know that the mome rath never lived that could outgrabe me? Yeah and furthermore I can become anything I want to; even if I were a warb, I wouldn't have to keep on being one if I didn't want to. I can become a playing card at will, too; once I was the jack of clubs, only I forgot to take my glasses off and some guy recognized me. I . . ."

Barney was backing slowly away, toward the petunia box at one end of the porch. His little blue eyes were wide. He saw

) 163 (

that I had him. "I think I go now," he said. And he walked
out into the rain. The rain followed him down the road.

I have a new hired man now. Barney never came back to
work for me after that day. Of course I figured out finally
what he meant about the garrick and the warbs: he had simply
got horribly mixed up in trying to tell me that he was going up
to the garret and clear out the wasps, of which I have thou-
sands. The new hired man is afraid of them. Barney could
have scooped them up in his hands and thrown them out a
window without getting stung. I am sure he trafficked with the
devil. But I am sorry I let him go.

XXVIII. The Remarkable Case of Mr. Bruhl

SAMUEL O. BRUHL was just an ordinary-looking citizen, like you and me, except for a curious, shoe-shaped scar on his left cheek, which he got when he fell against a wagon-tongue in his youth. He had a good job as treasurer for a syrup-and-fondant concern, a large, devout wife, two tractable daughters, and a nice home in Brooklyn. He worked from nine to five, took in a show occasionally, played a bad, complacent game of golf, and was usually in bed by eleven o'clock. The Bruhls had a dog named Bert, a small circle of friends, and an old sedan. They had made a comfortable, if unexciting, adjustment to life.

There was no reason in the world why Samuel Bruhl shouldn't have lived along quietly until he died of some commonplace malady. He was a man designed by Nature for an uneventful life, an inexpensive but respectable funeral, and a modest stone marker. All this you would have predicted had you observed his colorless comings and goings, his mild manner, the small stature of his dreams. He was, in brief, the sort of average citizen that observers of Judd Gray thought Judd Gray was. And precisely as that mild little family man was abruptly hurled into an incongruous tragedy, so was Samuel Bruhl suddenly picked out of the hundreds of men just like him and marked for an extravagant and unpredictable end. Oddly enough it was the shoe-shaped scar on his left cheek which brought to his heels a Nemesis he had never dreamed of. A blemish on his heart, a tic in his soul would have been different; one would have blamed Bruhl for whatever anguish an emotional or spiritual flaw laid him open to, but it is ironical indeed when the Furies ride down a man who has been guilty of nothing worse than an accident in his childhood.

Samuel O. Bruhl looked very much like George ("Shoescar") Clinigan. Clinigan had that same singular shoe-shaped scar on his left cheek. There was also a general resemblance in height, weight, and complexion. A careful study would have revealed very soon that Clinigan's eyes were shifty and Bruhl's eyes were clear, and that the syrup-and-fondant company's treasurer had a more pleasant mouth and a higher forehead than the gangster and racketeer, but at a glance the similarity was remarkable.

Had Clinigan not become notorious, this prank of Nature would never have been detected, but Clinigan did become notorious and dozens of persons observed that he looked like Bruhl. They saw Clinigan's picture in the papers the day he was shot, and the day after, and the day after that. Presently someone in the syrup-and-fondant concern mentioned to someone else that Clinigan looked like Mr. Bruhl, remarkably like Mr. Bruhl. Soon everybody in the place had commented on it, among themselves, and to Mr. Bruhl.

Mr. Bruhl rather laughed it off at first, but one day when Clinigan had been in the hospital a week, a cop peered closely at Mr. Bruhl when he was on his way home from work. After that, the little treasurer noticed a number of other strangers staring at him with mingled surprise and alarm. One small, dark man hastily thrust a hand into his coat pocket and paled slightly.

Mr. Bruhl began to worry. He began to imagine things. "I hope this fellow Clinigan doesn't pull through," he said one morning at breakfast. "He's a bad actor. He's better off dead."

"Oh, he'll pull through," said Mrs. Bruhl, who had been reading the morning paper. "It says here he'll pull through. But it says they'll shoot him again. It says they're sure to shoot him again."

The morning after the night that Clinigan left the hospital, secretly, by a side door, and disappeared into the town, Bruhl decided not to go to work. "I don't feel so good today," he said to his wife. "Would you call up the office and tell them I'm sick?"

"You don't look well," said his wife. "You really don't look well. Get down, Bert," she added, for the dog had jumped upon her lap and whined. The animal knew that something was wrong.

That evening Bruhl, who had mooned about the house all day, read in the papers that Clinigan had vanished, but was believed to be somewhere in the city. His various rackets required his presence, at least until he made enough money to skip out with; he had left the hospital penniless. Rival gangsters, the papers said, were sure to seek him out, to hunt him down, to give it to him again. "Give him what again?" asked Mrs. Bruhl when she read this. "Let's talk about something else," said her husband.

It was little Joey, the officeboy at the syrup-and-fondant company, who first discovered that Mr. Bruhl was afraid. Joey, who went about with tennis shoes on, entered the treasurer's office suddenly—flung open the door and started to say something. "Good God!" cried Mr. Bruhl, rising from his chair.

"Why, what's the matter, Mr. Bruhl?" asked Joey. Other little things happened. The switchboard girl phoned Mr. Bruhl's desk one afternoon and said there was a man waiting to see him, a Mr. Globe. "What's he look like?" asked Bruhl, who didn't know anybody named Globe. "He's small and dark," said the girl. "A small, dark man?" said Bruhl. "Tell him I'm out. Tell him I've gone to California." The personnel, comparing notes, decided at length that the treasurer was afraid of being mistaken for Shoescar and put on the spot. They said nothing to Mr. Bruhl about this, because they were forbidden to by Ollie Breithofter, a fattish clerk who was a tireless and inventive practical joker and who had an idea.

As the hunt went on for Clinigan and he still wasn't found and killed, Mr. Bruhl lost weight and grew extremely fidgety. He began to figure out new ways of getting to work, one requiring the use of two different ferry lines; he ate his lunch in, he wouldn't answer bells, he cried out when anyone dropped anything, and he ran into stores or banks when cruising taxi-drivers shouted at him. One morning, in setting the house to rights, Mrs. Bruhl found a revolver under his pillow. "I found a revolver under your pillow," she told him that night. "Burglars are bad in this neighborhood," he said. "You oughtn't to have a revolver," she said. They argued about it, he irritably, she uneasily, until time for bed. As Bruhl was undressing, after locking and bolting all the doors, the telephone rang. "It's for you, Sam," said Mrs. Bruhl. Her husband went slowly to the phone, passing Bert on the way. "I wish I was you," he said to the dog, and took up the receiver. "Get this, Shoescar," said a husky voice. "We trailed you where you are, see? You're cooked." The receiver at the other end was hung up. Bruhl shouted. His wife came running. "What is it, Sam, what is it?" she cried. Bruhl, pale, sick-looking, had fallen into a chair. "They got me," he moaned. "They got me." Slowly, deviously, Minnie Bruhl got it out of her husband that he had been mistaken for Clinigan and that he was cooked. Mrs. Bruhl was not very quick mentally, but she had a certain intuition and this intuition told her, as she trembled there in her nightgown above her broken husband, that this was the work of Ollie Breithofter. She instantly phoned Ollie Breithofter's wife and, before she hung up, had got the truth out of Mrs. Breithofter. It was Ollie who had called.

The treasurer of the Maskonsett Syrup & Fondant Company, Inc., was so relieved to know that the gangs weren't after him that he admitted frankly at the office next day that Ollie had fooled him for a minute. Mr. Bruhl even joined in the laughter and wisecracking, which went on all day. After that, for almost a week, the mild little man had comparative peace of mind. The papers said very little about Clinigan now. He had completely disappeared. Gang warfare had died down for the time being.

One Sunday morning Mr. Bruhl went for an automobile ride with his wife and daughters. They had driven about a mile through Brooklyn streets when, glancing in the mirror above his head, Mr. Bruhl observed a blue sedan just behind him. He turned off into the next side street, and the sedan turned off too. Bruhl made another turn, and the sedan followed him. "Where are you going, dear?" asked Mrs. Bruhl. Mr. Bruhl didn't answer her, he speeded up, he drove terrifically fast, he turned corners so wildly that the rear wheels swung around. A traffic cop shrilled at him. The younger daughter screamed. Bruhl drove right on, weaving in and out. Mrs. Bruhl began to berate him wildly. "Have you lost your mind, Sam?" she shouted. Mr. Bruhl looked behind him. The sedan was no longer to be seen. He slowed up. "Let's go home," he said. "I've had enough of this."

A month went by without incident (thanks largely to Mrs. Breithofter) and Samuel Bruhl began to be himself again. On the day that he was practically normal once more, Sluggy Pensiotta, alias Killer Lewis, alias Stranger Koetschke, was shot. Sluggy was the leader of the gang that had sworn to get Shoescar Clinigan. The papers instantly took up the gang-war story where they had left off. Pictures of Clinigan were published again. The slaying of Pensiotta, said the papers, meant but one thing: it meant that Shoescar Clinigan was cooked. Mr. Bruhl, reading this, went gradually to pieces once more.

After another week of skulking about, starting at every noise, and once almost fainting when an automobile backfired near him, Samuel Bruhl began to take on a remarkable new appearance. He talked out of the corner of his mouth, his eyes grew shifty. He looked more and more like Shoescar Clinigan. He snarled at his wife. Once he called her "Babe," and he had never called her anything but Minnie. He kissed her in a strange, new way, acting rough, almost brutal. At the office he was mean and overbearing. He used peculiar language. One night when the Bruhls had friends in for bridge—old Mr. Creegan and his wife—Bruhl suddenly appeared from upstairs with a pair of scarlet pajamas on, smoking a cigarette, and gripping his revolver. After a few loud and incoherent remarks of a boastful nature, he let fly at a clock on the mantel, and hit it squarely in the middle. Mrs. Bruhl screamed. Mr. Creegan fainted. Bert, who was in the kitchen, howled. "What's the matta you?" snarled Bruhl. "Ya bunch of softies."

Quite by accident, Mrs. Bruhl discovered, hidden away in a closet, eight or ten books on gangs and gangsters, which Bruhl had put there. They included "Al Capone," "You Can't Win," "10,000 Public Enemies" and a lot of others; and they were all well thumbed. Mrs. Bruhl realized that it was high time something was done, and she determined to have a doctor for her husband. For two or three days Bruhl had not gone to work. He lay around in his bedroom, in his red pajamas, smoking cigarettes. The office phoned once or twice. When Mrs. Bruhl urged him to get up and dress and go to work, he laughed and patted her roughly on the head. "It's a knockover, kid," he said. "We'll be sitting pretty. To hell with it."

The doctor who finally came and slipped into Bruhl's bedroom was very grave when he emerged. "This is a psychosis," he said, "a definite psychosis. Your husband is living in a world of fantasy. He has built up a curious defence mechanism against something or other." The doctor suggested that a psychiatrist be called in, but after he had gone Mrs. Bruhl decided to take her husband out of town on a trip. The Maskonsett Syrup & Fondant Company, Inc., was very fine about it. Mr. Scully said of course. "Sam is very valuable to us, Mrs. Bruhl," said Mr. Scully, "and we all hope he'll be all right." Just the same he had Mr. Bruhl's accounts examined, when Mrs. Bruhl had gone.

Oddly enough, Samuel Bruhl was amenable to the idea of going away. "I need a rest," he said. "You're right. Let's get the hell out of here." He seemed normal up to the time they set out for the Grand Central and then he insisted on leaving from the 125th Street station. Mrs. Bruhl took exception to this, as being ridiculous, whereupon her doting husband snarled at her. "God, what a dumb moll *I* picked," he said to Minnie Bruhl, and he added bitterly that if the heat was put to him it would be his own babe who was to blame. "And what do you think of *that*?" he said, pushing her to the floor of the cab.

They went to a little inn in the mountains. It wasn't a very nice place, but the rooms were clean and the meals were good. There was no form of entertainment, except a Tom Thumb golf course and an uneven tennis court, but Mr. Bruhl didn't mind. He said it was too cold outdoors, anyway. He stayed indoors, reading and smoking. In the evening he played the mechanical piano in the dining-room. He liked to play "More Than You Know" over and over again. One night, about nine o'clock, he was putting in his seventh or eighth nickel when four men walked into the dining-room. They were silent men, wearing overcoats, and carrying what appeared to be cases for musical instruments. They took out various kinds of guns from their cases, quickly, expertly, and walked over toward Bruhl, keeping step. He turned just in time to see them line up four abreast and aim at him. Nobody else was in the room. There was a cumulative roar and a series of flashes. Mr. Bruhl fell and the men walked out in single file, rapidly, nobody having said a word.

Mrs. Bruhl, state police, and the hotel manager tried to get the wounded man to talk. Chief Witznitz of the nearest town's police force tried it. It was no good. Bruhl only snarled and told them to go away and let him alone. Finally, Commissioner O'Donnell of the New York City Police Department arrived at the hospital. He asked Bruhl what the men looked like. "I don't know what they looked like," snarled Bruhl, "and if I did know I wouldn't tell you." He was silent a moment, then: "Cop!" he added, bitterly. The Commissioner sighed and turned away. "They're all like that," he said to the others in the room. "They never talk." Hearing this, Mr. Bruhl smiled, a pleased smile, and closed his eyes.

XXIX. Something to Say

Hugh Kingsmill and I stimulated each other to such a pitch that after the first meeting he had a brain storm and I lay sleepless all night and in the morning was on the brink of a nervous breakdown.—*William Gerhardi's "Memoirs of a Polyglot."*

ELLIOT VEREKER was always coming into and going out of my life. He was the only man who ever continuously stimulated me to the brink of a nervous breakdown. I met him first at a party in Amawalk, New York, on the Fourth of July, 1927. He arrived about noon in an old-fashioned horse cab, accompanied by a lady in black velvet whom he introduced as "my niece, Olga Nethersole." She was, it turned out, neither his niece nor Olga Nethersole. Vereker was a writer; he was gaunt and emaciated from sitting up all night talking; he wore an admiral's hat which he had stolen from an admiral. Usually he carried with him an old Gladstone bag filled with burned-out electric-light bulbs which it was his pleasure to throw, unexpectedly, against the sides of houses and the walls of rooms. He loved the popping sound they made and the tinkling sprinkle of fine glass that followed. He had an inordinate fondness for echoes. "Halloooo!" he would bawl, wherever he was, in a terrific booming voice that could have conjured up an echo on a prairie.

At the most inopportune and inappropriate moments he would snap out frank four-letter words, such as when he was talking to a little child or the sister of a vicar. He had no reverence and no solicitude. He would litter up your house, burn bedspreads and carpets with lighted cigarette stubs, and as likely as not depart with your girl and three or four of your most prized books and neckties. He was enamored of breaking phonograph records and phonographs; he liked to tear sheets and pillowcases in two; he would unscrew the doorknobs from your doors so that if you were in you couldn't get out and if you were out you couldn't get in. His was the true artistic fire, the rare gesture of genius. When I first met him, he was working on a novel entitled "Sue You Have Seen." He had worked it out, for some obscure reason, from the familiar expression "See you soon." He never finished it, nor did he ever finish, or indeed get very far with, any writing, but he was nevertheless, we all felt, one of the great original minds of our generation. That he had "something to say" was obvious in everything he did.

Vereker could converse brilliantly on literary subjects: Proust, Goethe, Voltaire, Whitman. Basically he felt for them a certain respect, but sometimes, and always when he was drunk, he would belittle their powers and their achievements in strong and pungent language. Proust, I later discovered, he had never read, but he made him seem more clear to me, and less important, than anybody else ever has. Vereker always liked to have an electric fan going while he talked and he would stick a folded newspaper into the fan so that the revolving blades scuttered against it, making a noise like the rattle of machine-gun fire. This exhilarated him and exhilarated me, too, but I suppose that it exhilarated him more than it did me. He seemed, at any rate, to get something out of it that I missed. He would raise his voice so that I could hear him above the racket. Sometimes, even then, I couldn't make out what he was saying.

"What?" I would shout. "You heard me!" he would yell, his good humor disappearing in an instant.

I had, of course, not heard him at all. There was no reasoning with him, no convincing him. I can still hear the musketry of those fans in my ears. They have done, I think, something to me. But for Vereker, and his great promise, one could endure a great deal. He would talk about the interests implicated in life, the coincidence of desire and realization, the symbols behind art and reality. He was fond of quoting Santayana when he was sober.

"Santayana," he would say when he was drinking, "has weight; he's a ton of feathers." Then he would laugh roaringly; if he was at Tony's, he would flounder out into the kitchen, insulting some movie critic on the way, and repeat his line to whoever was there, and come roaring back.

Vereker had a way of flinging himself at a sofa, kicking one end out of it; or he would drop into a fragile chair like a tired bird dog and something would crack. He never seemed to notice. You would invite him to dinner, or, what happened oftener, he would drop in for dinner uninvited, and while you were shaking up a cocktail in the kitchen he would disappear. He might go upstairs to wrench the bathtub away from the wall ("Breaking lead pipe is one of the truly enchanting adventures in life," he said once), or he might simply leave for good in one of those inexplicable huffs of his which were a sign of his peculiar genius. He was likely, of course, to come back around two in the morning bringing some awful woman with him, stirring up the fire, talking all night long, knocking things off tables, singing, or counting. I have known him to lie back on a sofa, his eyes closed, and count up to as high as twenty-four thousand by ones, in a bitter, snarling voice. It was his protest against the regularization of a mechanized age. "Achievement," he used to say, "is the fool's gold of idiots." He never believed in doing anything or in having anything done, either for the benefit of mankind or for individuals. He would have written, but for his philosophical indolence, very great novels indeed. We all knew that, and we treated him with a deference for which, now that he is gone, we are sincerely glad.

Once Vereker invited me to a house which a lady had turned over to him when she went to Paris for a divorce. (She expected to marry Vereker afterward but he would not marry her, nor would he move out of her house until she took legal action. "American women," Vereker would say, "are like American colleges: they have dull, half-dead faculties.") When I arrived at the house, Vereker chose to pretend that he did not remember me. It was rather difficult to carry the situation off, for he was in one of his black moods. It was then that he should have written, but never did; instead he would gabble brilliantly about other authors. "Goethe," he would say, "was a wax figure stuffed with hay. When you say that Proust was sick, you have said everything. Shakespeare was a dolt. If there had been no Voltaire, it would not have been necessary to create one." Etc. I had been invited for the weekend and I intended to stay; none of us ever left Vereker alone when we came upon him in one of his moods. He frequently threatened suicide and six or seven times attempted it but, in every case, there was someone on hand to prevent him. Once, I remember, he got me out of bed late at night at my own apartment. "I'm going through with it this time," he said, and darted into the bathroom. He was fumbling around for some poison in the medicine chest, which fortunately contained none, when I ran in and pleaded with him. "You have so many things yet to do," I said to him. "Yes," he said, "and so many people yet to insult." He talked brilliantly all night long, and drank up a bottle of cognac that I had got to send to my father.

I had gone to the bathroom for a shower, the time he invited me to his lady's house, when he stalked into the room. "Get out of that tub, you common housebreaker," he said, "or I shall summon the police!" I laughed, of course, and went on bathing. I was rubbing myself with a towel when the police arrived—he had sent for them! Vereker would have made an excellent actor; he convinced the police that he had never seen me before in his life. I was arrested, taken away, and locked up for the night. A few days later I got a note from Vereker. "I shall never ask you to my house again," he wrote, "after the way I acted last Saturday." His repentances, while whimsical, were always as complete as the erratic charades which called them forth. He was unpredictable and, at times, difficult, but he was always stimulating. Sometimes he keyed you up to a point beyond which, you felt, you could not go.

Vereker had a close escape from death once which I shall never forget. A famous American industrialist had invited a number of American writers and some visiting English men of letters out to his Long Island place. We were to make the trip in a huge bus that had been chartered for the purpose. Vereker came along and insisted, when we reached Long Island, on driving the bus. It was an icy night and he would put on the brakes at a curve, causing the heavy vehicle to skid ponderously. Several times we surged perilously near to a ditch and once the bus snapped off a big tree like a match. I remember that H. G. Bennett was along, and Arnold Wells, the three Sitwells, and four or five Waughs. One of them finally shut off the ignition and another struck Vereker over the head with a crank. His friends were furious. When the car stopped, we carried him outside and put him down on the hard, cold ground. Marvin Deane, the critic, held Vereker's head, which was bleeding profusely, in his lap, looked up at the busload of writers, and said: "You might have killed him! And he is a greater genius than any of you!" It was superb. Then the amazing Vereker opened his eyes. "That goes for me, too," he said, and closed them again.

We hurried him to a hospital, where, in two days, he was on his feet again; he left the hospital without a word to anybody, and we all chipped in to pay the bill. Vereker had some money at the time which his mother had given him but, as he said, he needed it. "I am glad he is up and out," I said to the nurse who had taken care of him. "So am I," she said. Vereker affected everybody the same way.

Some time after this we all decided to make up a fund and send Vereker to Europe to write. His entire output, I had discovered, consisted of only twenty or thirty pages, most of them bearing the round stain of liquor glasses; one page was the beginning of a play done more or less in the style of Gertrude Stein. It seemed to me as brilliant as anything of its kind.

We got together about fifteen hundred dollars and I was delegated to approach Vereker, as tactfully as possible. We knew that it was folly for him to go on the way he was, dissipating his talent; for weeks he had been in one of his blackest moods: he would call on people, drink up their rye, wrench light-brackets off the walls, hurl scintillating gibes at his friends and at the accepted literary masters of all time, through whose superficiality Vereker saw more clearly, I think, than anybody else I have ever known. He would end up by bursting into tears. "Here, but for the gracelessness of God," he would shout, "stands the greatest writer in the history of the world!" We felt that, despite Vereker's drunken exaggeration, there was more than a grain of truth in what he said: certainly nobody else we ever met had, so utterly, the fire of genius that blazed in Vereker, if outward manifestations meant anything.

He would never try for a Guggenheim fellowship. "Guggenheim follow-sheep!" he would snarl. "Fall in line, all you little men! Don't talk to me about Good-in-time fellowships!" He would go on that way, sparklingly, for an hour, his tirade finally culminating in one of those remarkable fits of temper in which he could rip up any apartment at all, no matter whose, in less than fifteen minutes.

Vereker, much to my surprise and gratification, took the fifteen hundred dollars without making a scene. I had suspected that he might denounce us all, that he might go into one of his brilliant philippics against Money, that he might even threaten again to take his life, for it had been several months since he had attempted suicide. But no; he snarled a bit, it is true, but he accepted the money. "I'm cheap at twice the price," he said.

It was the most money Vereker had ever had in his life and of course we should have known better than to let him have it all at once. The night of the day I gave it to him he cut a wide swath in the cheaper West Side night clubs and in Harlem, spent three hundred dollars, insulted several women, and figured in fist fights with a policeman, two taxi-drivers, and two husbands, all of whom won. We instantly decided to arrange his passage on a ship that was sailing for Cherbourg three nights later. Somehow or other we kept him out of trouble until the night of the sailing, when we gave a going-away party for him at Marvin Deane's house. Everybody was there: Gene Tunney, Sir Hubert Wilkins, Count von Luckner, Edward Bernays, and the literary and artistic crowd generally. Vereker got frightfully drunk. He denounced everybody at the party and also Hugh Walpole, Joseph Conrad, Crane, Henry James, Hardy, and Meredith. He dwelt on the subject of "Jude the Obscure." "Jude the Obscure," he would shout, "Jude the Obscene, June the Obscude, Obs the June Moon." He combined with his penetrating critical evaluations and his rare creative powers a certain unique fantasy not unlike that of Lewis Carroll. I once told him so. "Not unlike your goddam grandmother!" he screamed. He was sensitive; he hated to be praised to his face; and then of course he held the works of Carroll in a certain disesteem.

Thus the party went on. Everybody was speechless, spellbound, listening to Elliot Vereker. You could not miss his force. He was always the one person in a room. When it got to be eleven o'clock, I felt that we had better round up Vereker and start for the docks, for the boat sailed at midnight. He was nowhere to be found. We were alarmed. We searched every room, looked under beds, and into closets, but he was gone. Some of us ran downstairs and out into the street, asking cab-drivers and passersby if they had seen him, a gaunt, tall, wild man with his hair in his eyes. Nobody had. It was almost eleven-thirty when somebody thought to look on the roof, to which there was access by a ladder through a trapdoor. Vereker was there. He lay sprawled on his face, the back of his head crushed in by a blow from some heavy instrument, probably a bottle. He was quite dead. "The world's loss," murmured Deane, as he looked down at the pitiful dust so lately the most burning genius we had ever been privileged to know, "is Hell's gain."

I think we all felt that way.

XXX. Snapshot of a Dog

I RAN across a dim photogragh of him the other day, going through some old things. He's been dead twenty-five years. His name was Rex (my two brothers and I named him when we were in our early teens) and he was a bull terrier. "An American bull terrier," we used to say, proudly; none of your English bulls. He had one brindle eye that sometimes made him look like a clown and sometimes reminded you of a politician with derby hat and cigar. The rest of him was white except for a brindle saddle that always seemed to be slipping off and a brindle stocking on a hind leg. Nevertheless, there was a nobility about him. He was big and muscular and beautifully made. He never lost his dignity even when trying to accomplish the extravagant tasks my brothers and myself used to set for him. One of these was the bringing of a ten-foot wooden rail into the yard through the back gate. We would throw it out into the alley and tell him to go get it. Rex was as powerful as a wrestler, and there were not many things that he couldn't manage somehow to get hold of with his great jaws and lift or drag to wherever he wanted to put them, or wherever we wanted them put. He would catch the rail at the balance and lift it clear of the ground and trot with great confidence toward the gate. Of course, since the gate was only four feet wide or so, he couldn't bring the rail in broadside. He found that out when he got a few terrific jolts, but he wouldn't give up. He finally figured out how to do it, by dragging the rail, holding onto one end, growling. He got a great, wagging satisfaction out of his work. We used to bet kids who had never seen Rex in action that he could catch a baseball thrown as high as they could throw it. He almost never let us down. Rex could hold a baseball with ease in his mouth, in one cheek, as if it were a chew of tobacco.

He was a tremendous fighter, but he never started fights. I don't believe he liked to get into them, despite the fact that he came from a line of fighters. He never went for another dog's throat but for one of its ears (that teaches a dog a lesson), and he would get his grip, close his eyes, and hold on. He could hold on for hours. His longest fight lasted from dusk until almost pitch-dark, one Sunday. It was fought in East Main Street in Columbus with a large, snarly nondescript that belonged to a big colored man. When Rex finally got his ear grip, the brief whirlwind of snarling turned to screeching. It was frightening to listen to and to watch. The Negro boldly picked the dogs up somehow and began swinging them around his head, and finally let them fly like a hammer in a hammer throw, but although they landed ten feet away with a great plump, Rex still held on.

The two dogs eventually worked their way to the middle of the car tracks, and after a while two or three streetcars were held up by the fight. A motorman tried to pry Rex's jaws open with a switch rod; somebody lighted a fire and made a torch of a stick and held that to Rex's tail, but he paid no attention.

In the end, all the residents and storekeepers in the neighborhood were on hand, shouting this, suggesting that. Rex's joy of battle, when battle was joined, was almost tranquil. He had a kind of pleasant expression during fights, not a vicious one, his eyes closed in what would have seemed to be sleep had it not been for the turmoil of the struggle. The Oak Street Fire Department finally had to be sent for—I don't know why nobody thought of it sooner. Five or six pieces of apparatus arrived, followed by a battalion chief. A hose was attached and a powerful stream of water was turned on the dogs. Rex held on for several moments more while the torrent buffeted him about like a log in a freshet. He was a hundred yards away from where the fight started when he finally let go.

The story of that Homeric fight got all around town, and some of our relatives looked upon the incident as a blot on the family name. They insisted that we get rid of Rex, but we were very happy with him, and nobody could have made us give him up. We would have left town with him first, along any road there was to go. It would have been different, perhaps, if he had ever started fights, or looked for trouble. But he had a gentle disposition. He never bit a person in the ten strenuous years that he lived, nor ever growled at anyone except prowlers. He killed cats, that is true, but quickly and neatly and without especial malice, the way men kill certain animals. It was the only thing he did that we could never cure him of doing. He never killed, or even chased, a squirrel. I don't know why. He had his own philosophy about such things. He never ran barking after wagons or automobiles. He didn't seem to see the idea in pursuing something you couldn't catch, or something you couldn't do anything with, even if you did catch it. A wagon was one of the things he couldn't tug along with his mighty jaws, and he knew it. Wagons, therefore, were not a part of his world.

Swimming was his favorite recreation. The first time he ever saw a body of water (Alum Creek), he trotted nervously along the steep bank for a while, fell to barking wildly, and finally plunged in from a height of eight feet or more. I shall always remember that shining, virgin dive. Then he swam upstream and back just for the pleasure of it, like a man. It was fun to see him battle upstream against a stiff current, struggling and growling every foot of the way. He had as much fun in the water as any person I have known. You didn't have to throw a stick in the water to get him to go in. Of course, he would bring back a stick to you if you did throw one in. He would even have brought back a piano if you had thrown one in.

That reminds me of the night, way after midnight, when he went a-roving in the light of the moon and brought back a small chest of drawers that he found somewhere—how far from the house nobody ever knew; since it was Rex, it could easily have been half a mile. There were no drawers in the chest when he got it home, and it wasn't a good one—he hadn't taken it out of anybody's house; it was just an old cheap piece that somebody had abandoned on a trash heap. Still, it was something he wanted, probably because it presented a nice problem in transportation. It tested his mettle. We first knew about his achievement when, deep in the night, we heard him trying to get the chest up onto the porch. It sounded as if two or three people were trying to tear the house down. We came downstairs and turned on the porch light. Rex was on the top step trying to pull the thing up, but it had caught somehow and he was just holding his own. I suppose he would have held his own till dawn if we hadn't helped him. The next day we carted the chest miles away and threw it out. If we had thrown it out in a nearby alley, he would have brought it home again, as a small token of his integrity in such matters. After all, he had been taught to carry heavy wooden objects about, and he was proud of his prowess.

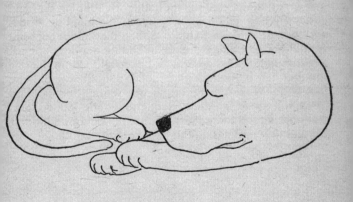

I am glad Rex never saw a trained police dog jump. He was just an amateur jumper himself, but the most daring and tenacious I have ever seen. He would take on any fence we pointed out to him. Six feet was easy for him, and he could do eight by making a tremendous leap and hauling himself over finally by his paws, grunting and straining; but he lived and died without knowing that twelve- and sixteen-foot walls were too much for him. Frequently, after letting him try to go over one for a while, we would have to carry him home. He would never have given up trying.

There was in his world no such thing as the impossible. Even death couldn't beat him down. He died, it is true, but only, as one of his admirers said, after "straight-arming the death angel" for more than an hour. Late one afternoon he wandered home, too slowly and too uncertainly to be the Rex that had trotted briskly homeward up our avenue for ten years. I think we all knew when he came through the gate that he was dying. He had apparently taken a terrible beating, probably from the owner of some dog that he had got into a fight with. His head and body were scarred. His heavy collar with the teeth marks of many a battle on it was awry; some of the big brass studs in it were sprung loose from the leather. He licked at our hands and, staggering, fell, but got up again. We could see that he was looking for someone. One of his three masters was not home. He did not get home for an hour. During that hour the bull terrier fought against death as he had fought against the cold, strong current of Alum Creek, as he had fought to climb twelve-foot walls. When the person he was waiting for did come through the gate, whistling, ceasing to whistle, Rex walked a few wabbly paces toward him, touched his hand with his muzzle, and fell down again. This time he didn't get up.

XXXI. The Evening's at Seven

HE HADN'T lighted the upper light in his office all afternoon and now he turned out the desk lamp. It was a quarter of seven in the evening and it was dark and raining. He could hear the rattle of taxicabs and trucks and the sound of horns. Very far off a siren screamed its frenzied scream and he thought: it's a little like an anguish dying with the years. When it gets to Third Avenue, or Ninety-fifth Street, he thought, I won't hear it any more.

I'll be home, he said to himself, as he got up slowly and slowly put on his hat and overcoat (the overcoat was damp), by seven o'clock, if I take a taxicab, I'll say hello, my dear, and the two yellow lamps will be lighted and my papers will be on my desk, and I'll say I guess I'll lie down a few minutes before dinner, and she will say all right and ask two or three small questions about the day and I'll answer them.

When he got outside of his office, in the street, it was dark and raining and he lighted a cigarette. A young man went by whistling loudly. Two girls went by talking gaily, as if it were not raining, as if this were not a time for silence and for remembering. He called to a taxicab and it stopped and he got in, and sat there, on the edge of the seat, and the driver finally said where to? He gave a number he was thinking about.

She was surprised to see him and, he believed, pleased. It was very nice to be in her apartment again. He faced her, quickly, and it seemed to him as if he were facing somebody in a tennis game. She would want to know (but wouldn't ask) why he was, so suddenly, there, and he couldn't exactly say: I gave a number to a taxi-driver and it was your number. He couldn't say that; and besides, it wasn't that simple.

It was dark in the room and still raining outside. He lighted a cigarette (not wanting one) and looked at her. He watched her lovely gestures as of old and she said he looked tired and he said he wasn't tired and he asked her what she had been doing and she said oh, nothing much. He talked, sitting awkwardly on the edge of a chair, and she talked, lying gracefully on a chaise-longue, about people they had known and hadn't cared about. He was mainly conscious of the rain outside and of the soft darkness in the room and of other rains and other darknesses. He got up and walked around the room looking at pictures but not seeing what they were, and realizing that some old familiar things gleamed darkly, and he came abruptly face to face with something he had given her, a trivial and comic thing, and it didn't seem trivial or comic now, but very large and important and embarrassing, and he turned away from it and asked after somebody else he didn't care about. Oh, she said, and this and that and so and such (words he wasn't listening to). Yes, he said, absently, I suppose so. Very much, he said (in answer to something else), very much. Oh, she said, laughing at him, not *that* much! He didn't have any idea what they were talking about.

She asked him for a cigarette and he walked over and gave her one, not touching her fingers but very conscious of her fingers. He was remembering a twilight when it had been raining and dark, and he thought of April and kissing and laughter. He noticed a clock on the mantel and it was ten after seven. She said you never used to believe in clocks. He laughed and looked at her for a time and said I have to be at the hotel by seven-thirty, or I don't get anything to eat; it's that sort of hotel. Oh, she said.

He walked to a table and picked up a figurine and set it down again with extreme care, looking out of the corner of his eye at the trivial and comic and gigantic present he had given her. He wondered if he would kiss her and when he would kiss her and if she wanted to be kissed and if she were thinking of it, but she asked him what he would have to eat tonight at his hotel. He said clam chowder. Thursday, he said, they always have clam chowder. Is that the way you know it's Thursday, she said, or is that the way you know it's clam chowder?

He picked up the figurine and put it down again, so that he could look (without her seeing him look) at the clock. It was eighteen minutes after seven and he had the mingled thoughts clocks gave him. You mustn't, she said, miss your meal. (She remembered he hated the word meal.) He turned around quickly and went over quickly and sat beside her and took hold of one of her fingers and she looked at the finger and not at him and he looked at the finger and not at her, both of them as if it were a new and rather remarkable thing.

He got up suddenly and picked up his hat and coat and as suddenly put them down again and took two rapid determined steps toward her, and her eyes seemed a little wider. A bell rang. Oh that, she said, will be Clarice. And they relaxed. He looked a question and she said: my sister; and he said oh, of course. In a minute it was Clarice like a small explosion in the dark and rainy day talking rapidly of this and that: my dear he and this awful and then of all people so nothing loth and I said and he said, if you can imagine that! He picked up his hat and coat and Clarice said hello to him and he said hello and looked at the clock and it was almost twenty-five after seven.

She went to the door with him looking lovely, and it was lovely and dark and raining outside and he laughed and she laughed and she was going to say something but he went out into the rain and waved back at her (not wanting to wave back at her) and she closed the door and was gone. He lighted a cigarette and let his hand get wet in the rain and the cigarette get wet and rain dripped from his hat. A taxicab drove up and the driver spoke to him and he said: what? and: oh, sure. And now he was going home.

He was home by seven-thirty, almost exactly, and he said good evening to old Mrs. Spencer (who had the sick husband), and good evening to old Mrs. Holmes (who had the sick Pomeranian), and he nodded and smiled and presently he was sitting at his table and the waitress spoke to him. She said: the Mrs. will be down, won't she? and he said yes, she will. And the waitress said clam chowder tonight, and consommé: you always take the clam chowder, ain't I right? No, he said, I'll have the consommé.

XXXII. Smashup

WHEN Tommy Trinway was fifteen years old, he knocked a lamp off the family surrey trying to drive it, behind the old family mare, Maud, into Bitzer's livery stable in Columbus. Maud, nearing bed and board, had trotted up suddenly, jerking one rein from young Trinway's hands, and as a result she had veered to the left and a lamp had been knocked off the carriage as it entered the stable. That happened a long time ago—it was in 1909—but it had had a lasting effect on Tommy. He was not allowed to drive Maud after that—Maud, who was fat-bellied and gentle and sixteen—but his younger brother Ned could drive her, and that had had an effect on Tommy, too. He took to reading books instead of going out and playing games with the fellows. His mother worried about him.

When the Trinways bought a Rambler, Tommy's old accident with the carriage rose out of his past to plague him. He was nineteen then, but everybody said he was too nervous to drive the Rambler. Tommy didn't insist. He was afraid to drive the Rambler. He would dream at night of driving it, sometimes with his cap on backward, at sixty miles an hour, like Barney Oldfield; but mostly he would dream of driving it into the sides of buildings and off the tops of buildings. Once in a while, at breakfast, Tommy would reach the verge of announcing that he was going to learn to drive the auto—you were somebody in those days if your family had a Rambler and you drove it—but his big moment would always pass, his courage would wear off, and he never asserted himself. He became a studious young man, a young man of thought and not of action. Once he had played tennis with some ability, and more promise, and he had been a fair dancer, too, but he seldom played tennis any more—when he did, Ned beat him—and he never went to dances. His mother still worried about him, but nobody else did. He was looked upon as a sedentary young man, a natural born student.

Tommy became slightly bald in his twenties and he took to wearing glasses, but he was not unattractive. At least, he was not unattractive to Betty Carter. She fell in love with him. She felt that there was something deep, if not profound, behind Tommy's moody silences, and the way he wrinkled his brow, and his slow, uncertain smile. She got him to go to dances again once in a while, and she told him she liked the way he danced. She decided that he had a future. Tommy brightened somewhat under Betty's admiration. When he was twenty-eight, she married him.

Tommy Trinway did not want to drive the car his wife picked out for him to buy. But he bought it and he learned to drive it. He would practice in the early morning in a park at the edge of town (never with Betty, though; he didn't want her to see him groping and fumbling). He got so he could drive well enough, but he never liked it. He was always uneasy in traffic. Drivers of cars behind him would sound their klaxons

irritably, and sometimes shout at him as they roared past on his left. Now and then, seeing in his mirror a big car rushing up behind, he would signal it on, slow down, and pull over to the side of the road. Betty used to laugh at him for that and call him silly. Pleasantly enough—at first. She drove very fast herself, with keen concentration, quick reflexes, and evident enjoyment. Tommy would find himself studying her, when she was driving. There was an assured set to her mouth and a certain glint in her eyes. It dismayed him slightly.

Betty finally took over the driving of the car entirely. Tommy began to get in the seat beside the driver's seat after the day in Broad Street when he absently put the gears in reverse and banged into a Pierce-Arrow parked behind him. He sat puzzled and helpless until Betty said firmly, "Let me get at the wheel." He moved over and let her get at the wheel. After that, Betty drove wherever they went. The more she drove, the faster she drove. She was always whirling out of line to pass cars ahead. Tommy lived in dread of a head-on collision, and sometimes Betty would become conscious of his tenseness. "Don't be so silly," she would say to him. "You're jumpy as a cat." When the gibe was new, he would laugh, and say something funny, maybe, and sometimes, after a moment, she would pat him on the shoulder. But it got so that he didn't answer her, and she kept both hands on the wheel.

Betty sprained her left wrist—the first accident she had had in their ten years of married life—the summer they spent at West Dennis, on the Cape. "You're going to *have* to drive now," she told Tommy. "Sure," he said. "Sure. I'll drive." But he was silent at mealtimes and he looked miserable. He kept thinking of the day when he had gone out to the garage in Betty's absence and tried to back the car out and drive it around a little. She had gone somewhere in the Laytons' car to play tennis. Tommy had been thirty-nine years old that day, and something about being thirty-nine had made him determined to go out and drive the car. He started the engine after some trouble (he forgot for a while to switch on the ignition) and practiced shifting gears. He found himself trembling just doing that, and when he accidentally pressed his wrist on the klaxon button and it screamed at him, he jumped and took his foot off the clutch, and the car leaped forward and shook him up a bit before the engine choked and died. He hadn't told Betty about the incident. Once she would merely have laughed about it; but she wouldn't now, he thought.

In the days before they were to start to New York, Tommy would take the car out on the roads early in the morning, before there was much traffic. He managed fairly well, but his coordination was slow, and once or twice he put the brake on hard without letting his clutch out and killed the engine. That would give him a sense of helplessness and panic, and he would sit for a long time without starting the engine again, remembering the time he had knocked the lamp off the surrey. He had hated Bitzer, he reflected, recalling the livery-stable man perfectly—a stumpy, bow-legged man with a beard. Tommy had not told the family about that accident when he went home. They had found out about it the next morning from Bitzer. Tommy had been afraid to tell the family, just as he had been afraid to tell Betty about trying to back the car out of the garage.

One morning when he was out practicing driving, he came to a wide, straight concrete road, and pretty soon, to his own surprise, he had the car up to fifty miles an hour, and then fifty-five, and then sixty. He kept it at sixty for a little while, and as he roared along he suddenly began to chant loudly, for some crazy reason, "Little Bet-ty Bit-zer, little Bet-ty Bit-zer!" Then he slowed down as abruptly as he had started up, and stopped chanting. He felt pretty good when he drove back to the house and got breakfast. "The coffee is too strong," said Betty. "The coffee is swell," he told her. She widened her eyes. "Well!" she said. "Old cocksure!" Their laughter was a little strained, like the laughter of two people who have just met.

The day that he started to drive the car to New York, with his wife beside him, Tommy Trinway felt vaguely that his future with her lay before him on the roads, obscure and ominous. He drove steadily, a little stiffly, and not fast. Other cars complained briefly, and roared past. Once in a while, when Tommy wavered, Betty would start up and make as if to grab the wheel, but she didn't. "Well!" she would begin, impatiently, and stop. They went along most of the time in silence. When, after many hours of driving and more stops than Betty thought were necessary, Tommy came out of the quiet of the Hutchinson River Parkway into the clangor and tangle of Fordham and felt the menace of the Bronx ahead of him, he almost drove to one side and stopped, but he didn't; he kept on, slowly. He was tired and worn. He had driven a long way, over good roads and over narrow, twisting roads. His shoulders ached from leaning tensely forward. The Bronx loomed up before him, like an ether nightmare he had had as a boy. Only there had been, that time, finally oblivion, and here now were unending shouts and banging, and the roaring of elevated trains overhead, and a snarl of broad, ugly streets curving off in every direction, and big, sweaty women pushing baby carriages, and scowling men in shirt sleeves jabbering, and trucks rumbling and pounding by, and taxis rushing around him, and lights turning red and green under their iron hoods, and policemen making formidable gestures with their huge hands.

He got through it somehow. Once a cop blew a series of quick, petulant blasts on his whistle and Betty snapped, "Speed it up! You're blocking people!" and he had speeded up, narrowly missing the front fender of a laundry truck, whose driver shouted some profanity at him. "I wish I could take that wheel,"

Betty said. Tommy's heart was beating painfully in his throat and he didn't answer. Betty had to tell him which turns to make all the way. Once she cried, "Good God, watch the *lights*!" He finally reached the entrance to Central Park at 110th Street. As they drove through the Park, she settled back and sighed. "Well, we're going to make it alive, I guess," she said. "Yeah," said Tommy, tightly. "For heaven's sake, relax a little," she told him. "I'm all right," said Tommy, with an effort at sharpness that failed. He wasn't all right.

It was at Sixth Avenue and Forty-seventh Street that doom shot out in front of his car. The doom of an angular woman of sixty, the doom of Tommy and Betty. It happened in a flash. The woman had reached the line of "L" pillars nearer the east curb and was hovering there uncertainly, waiting to cross to the west curb. A taxi going north whisked by her and she saw that no other car was close behind it. She darted into the path of Tommy's car, coming the other way. He had a quick, hot sense of horror, buildings and people writhed around him, the brakes of cars screamed. Then all the noises of the city stopped. Everything stopped. "Nice piece of drivin', mister," a voice was saying, and Tommy looked up at a policeman standing beside the door of his car. The policeman walked toward the back of the car, and Tommy opened the door and leaned out and followed him with his eyes. A man was supporting the angular old woman. She was grinning idiotically. "I guess she's all right," the man told the policeman. "I seen it. He didn't hit her. He just grazed her." "You're lucky, lady," said the policeman. "You can thank your stars that fella can drive like that. You wanta stay on the sidewalk when you see that red light. This street ain't no playgrounds." Cars began to sound their klaxons and a streetcar bell clanged. The cop motioned to Tommy to back up. Tommy saw then, for the first time, that he had whirled his car sharply to the right and had come to a stop only a few inches from an "L" pillar. "We just barely grazed her," said Betty. "The crazy fool." Tommy started to back up. "Take the emergency brake off," said Betty. Tommy frowned and let the brake forward. He backed up and straightened out and went on. "Close call, buddy," said a grinning taxi-driver, passing him.

"I guess I rate a drink," said Tommy, as they went into the lobby of their hotel. He had turned the car over to the doorman with a proud sigh. Something heavy had dropped away from him. "I guess we both rate a drink," said Betty. They sat down in big chairs in a corner and ordered Scotch and soda. Tommy stretched his legs languidly. "Well," he said, "nobody got killed." "No, thank God," said Betty. "But somebody *would* have if I hadn't jerked on the hand brake. You never think of the hand brake. You'd have hit that pillar sure, and killed both of us." Tommy looked at her coldly. "Oh, *yeah?*" he said. She raised her eyebrows in surprise and indignation at his tone; the match she was about to hold to her cigarette went out. "What's the matter with you?" she asked. The waiter brought their drinks, put them down, and went away. "Nothing is the matter with me," said Tommy. "I'm fine." She stared at her husband over the cigarette and, striking another match, still stared. He stared back at her. He tossed off his Scotch with a new, quick gesture, set the glass down, got up, and lounged over to the desk. "We'll want two single rooms tonight, Mr. Brent," he said to the man at the desk. Mr. Brent looked over his glasses in some surprise as Tommy signed the register and then walked jauntily out the revolving doors into the street, whistling.

XXXIII. The Man on the Train

I INSTANTLY felt as if I had stumbled into a wrong apartment in which someone was dressing. And yet I had merely glanced across the aisle of a train at a man I had never seen before, who looked back at me. I had the quick, unreasonable feeling that there must be something I could do for him. It was almost as if he had spoken. And yet I met his gaze for only a moment or two and then we both turned away. It happened a long time ago—four or five years—and it is as meaningless to my life as an old forgotten telephone number; but there it is, as sharp as any memory I have of a friend. It comes up before me, clear, irrelevant, and uncalled for, at unexpected hours.

I had never seen the man before and I would not recognize him if I saw him again. I couldn't tell you the color of the suit he wore, or how large he was, or even whether he had a hat on. All that is gone, like the roads and rains and houses that whisk past you when you are riding on a train; the man as a person is as lost to me as the lonely figures that wave at you from fields when your train goes by. But I remember his eyes as well as I remember anything.

There is something lugubrious about the expression of a man with a toothache. I think I could always pick out such a sufferer instantly: a man with a toothache looks, crazily enough, as if he were trying not to laugh. But this was not a look of physical pain. I felt, for some odd reason, as if the cause for it were on the tip of my mind; as if, by some little extra effort, I could divine the dark experience, whatever it was.

I remember it was a fine afternoon in April or May. I had walked to the Grand Central and bought some brightly covered magazines, and I had slumped down comfortably in a rear coach, and a dozen women without faces came into the coach, and a dozen men who were merely suits of clothes. I was only vaguely conscious of them, as movement and murmuring; but I became acutely aware of him. He had made no sign of any kind, I had not yet seen him, but I was aware of him as one becomes aware on entering a room that one's name has just been spoken there.

I looked up finally, under a kind of compulsion, and saw him. He was not looking at me. He was sitting tensely on the edge of the seat across the aisle, one hand lying limply on his knee, the other clutching tightly the back of the seat in front of him. The train hadn't yet begun to move out of the darkness and closeness of the Grand Central cavern. I had the feeling that the man wanted to jump up and get off the train, run off; but he just sat there, one hand clutching the seat-back, the other lying limply on his knee. He turned his head and looked at me. I didn't look at him again all during the ride.

The people on the coach thinned out at every stop, moving heavily, without energy, through the aisle; seeming sodden and damp although it was a bright dry afternoon. One man sitting in front of me, with his head lolling back, snored raspingly. I tried to read, but couldn't. I was too conscious of the man across the aisle, still sitting, I was certain, as he had been before the train started—as if he were about to get up and protest against something, some incredible thing that was about to come to pass. But he didn't get up; I don't believe he ever relaxed, or made any movement at all, except when the conductor stopped to take up his ticket. I thought the conductor spoke to him, a sentence or two, but I didn't hear the man answer. The conductor went slowly on.

It was a bright sunny trip and I became drowsy after South Norwalk, but I couldn't sleep; the man stuck too keenly in my consciousness. I don't know just where he got off, but after a time I felt that he was no longer there. The tension and uncomfortableness went out of me. I had closed my eyes, but I opened them and began to leaf through a magazine. When I glanced furtively across the aisle, I saw that he had gone. There was only the snoring man, deeper in dream now, and a woman's hat peeking over the back of a seat far in front of me. I began to feel a little foolish about my awareness of the man who had gone. I had probably exaggerated the whole thing: made catastrophe out of predicament.

The train whistled for my station. I think I would have dismissed the man from my mind if the conductor had not come back through the coach, saying something in a disinterested drone about not forgetting your parcels. I was standing up, gathering my magazines together, trying to decide which ones to leave, when he stopped beside me. He was one of those gray-haired, placid conductors who seem beyond excitement, impervious to concern of any kind. I don't know why he felt impelled to speak to me, but apparently he did. It is a little startling when a conductor begins talking to you about something unconnected with tickets, or towns, or time. "Ja notice that fella was sittin' opposite you?" he asked me. He indicated the seat the man had sat in. "Poor fella just lost his little girl," he said.

XXXIV. The Greatest Man in the World

Looking back on it now, from the vantage point of 1940, one can only marvel that it hadn't happened long before it did. The United States of America had been, ever since Kitty Hawk, blindly constructing the elaborate petard by which, sooner or later, it must be hoist. It was inevitable that some day there would come roaring out of the skies a national hero of insufficient intelligence, background, and character successfully to endure the mounting orgies of glory prepared for aviators who stayed up a long time or flew a great distance. Both Lindbergh and Byrd, fortunately for national decorum and international amity, had been gentlemen; so had our other famous aviators. They wore their laurels gracefully, withstood the awful weather of publicity, married excellent women, usually of fine family, and quietly retired to private life and the enjoyment of their varying fortunes. No untoward incidents, on a worldwide scale, marred the perfection of their conduct on the perilous heights of fame. The exception to the rule was, however, bound o occur and it did, in July, 1937, when Jack ("Pal") Smurch, erstwhile mechanic's helper in a small garage in Westfield, Iowa, flew a second-hand, single-motored Bresthaven Dragon-Fly III monoplane all the way around the world, without stopping.

Never before in the history of aviation had such a flight as Smurch's ever been dreamed of. No one had even taken seriously the weird floating auxiliary gas tanks, invention of the mad New Hampshire professor of astronomy, Dr. Charles Lewis Gresham, upon which Smurch placed full reliance. When the garage worker, a slightly built, surly, unprepossessing young man of twenty-two, appeared at Roosevelt Field early in July, 1937, slowly chewing a great quid of scrap tobacco, and announced "Nobody ain't seen no flyin' yet," the newspapers touched briefly and satirically upon his projected twenty-five-thousand-mile flight. Aëronautical and automotive experts dismissed the idea curtly, implying that it was a hoax, a publicity stunt. The rusty, battered, second-hand plane wouldn't go. The Gresham auxiliary tanks wouldn't work. It was simply a cheap joke.

Smurch, however, after calling on a girl in Brooklyn who worked in the flap-folding department of a large paper-box factory, a girl whom he later described as his "sweet patootie," climbed nonchalantly into his ridiculous plane at dawn of the memorable seventh of July, 1937, spit a curve of tobacco juice into the still air, and took off, carrying with him only a gallon of bootleg gin and six pounds of salami.

When the garage boy thundered out over the ocean the papers were forced to record, in all seriousness, that a mad, unknown young man—his name was variously misspelled—had actually set out upon a preposterous attempt to span the world in a rickety, one-engined contraption, trusting to the long-distance refuelling device of a crazy schoolmaster. When, nine days later,

without having stopped once, the tiny plane appeared above San
Francisco Bay, headed for New York, spluttering and choking,
to be sure, but still magnificently and miraculously aloft, the
headlines, which long since had crowded everything else off the
front page—even the shooting of the Governor of Illinois by
the Vileti gang—swelled to unprecedented size, and the news
stories began to run to twenty-five and thirty columns. It was
noticeable, however, that the accounts of the epoch-making
flight touched rather lightly upon the aviator himself. This was
not because facts about the hero as a man were too meagre, but
because they were too complete.

Reporters, who had been rushed out to Iowa when Smurch's
plane was first sighted over the little French coast town of
Serly-le-Mer, to dig up the story of the great man's life, had
promptly discovered that the story of his life could not be
printed. His mother, a sullen short-order cook in a shack restaurant on the edge of a tourists' camping ground near Westfield, met all inquiries as to her son with an angry "Ah, the
hell with him; I hope he drowns." His father appeared to be
in jail somewhere for stealing spotlights and laprobes from
tourists' automobiles; his young brother, a weak-minded lad,
had but recently escaped from the Preston, Iowa, Reformatory
and was already wanted in several Western towns for the theft
of money-order blanks from post offices. These alarming dis-
coveries were still piling up at the very time that Pal Smurch,
the greatest hero of the twentieth century, blear-eyed, dead for
sleep, half-starved, was piloting his crazy junk-heap high above
the region in which the lamentable story of his private life was
being unearthed, headed for New York and a greater glory
than any man of his time had ever known.

The necessity for printing some account in the papers of the
young man's career and personality had led to a remarkable
predicament. It was of course impossible to reveal the facts, for
a tremendous popular feeling in favor of the young hero had

sprung up, like a grass fire, when he was halfway across Europe on his flight around the globe. He was, therefore, described as a modest chap, taciturn, blond, popular with his friends, popular with girls. The only available snapshot of Smurch, taken at the wheel of a phony automobile in a cheap photo studio at an amusement park, was touched up so that the little vulgarian looked quite handsome. His twisted leer was smoothed into a pleasant smile. The truth was, in this way, kept from the youth's ecstatic compatriots; they did not dream that the Smurch family was despised and feared by its neighbors in the obscure Iowa town, nor that the hero himself, because of numerous unsavory exploits, had come to be regarded in Westfield as a nuisance and a menace. He had, the reporters discovered, once knifed the principal of his high school—not mortally, to be sure, but he had knifed him; and on another occasion, surprised in the act of stealing an altarcloth from a church, he had bashed the sacristan over the head with a pot of Easter lilies; for each of these offences he had served a sentence in the reformatory.

Inwardly, the authorities, both in New York and in Washington, prayed that an understanding Providence might, however awful such a thing seemed, bring disaster to the rusty, battered plane and its illustrious pilot, whose unheard-of flight had aroused the civilized world to hosannas of hysterical praise. The authorities were convinced that the character of the renowned aviator was such that the limelight of adulation was bound to reveal him, to all the world, as a congenital hooligan mentally and morally unequipped to cope with his own prodigious fame. "I trust," said the Secretary of State, at one of many secret Cabinet meetings called to consider the national dilemma, "I trust that his mother's prayer will be answered," by which he referred to Mrs. Emma Smurch's wish that her son might be drowned. It was, however, too late for that— Smurch had leaped the Atlantic and then the Pacific as if they were millponds. At three minutes after two o'clock on the after-

oon of July 17, 1937, the garage boy brought his idiotic plane
to Roosevelt Field for a perfect three-point landing.

It had, of course, been out of the question to arrange a modest
ttle reception for the greatest flier in the history of the world.
Ie was received at Roosevelt Field with such elaborate and pre-
ntious ceremonies as rocked the world. Fortunately, however,
e worn and spent hero promptly swooned, had to be removed
odily from his plane, and was spirited from the field without
aving opened his mouth once. Thus he did not jeopardize the
ignity of this first reception, a reception illumined by the pres-
ace of the Secretaries of War and the Navy, Mayor Michael J.
Ioriarity of New York, the Premier of Canada, Governors Fan-
iman, Groves, McFeely, and Critchfield, and a brilliant array
f European diplomats. Smurch did not, in fact, come to in time
 take part in the gigantic hullabaloo arranged at City Hall for
e next day. He was rushed to a secluded nursing home and
onfined in bed. It was nine days before he was able to get up,
r to be more exact, before he was permitted to get up. Mean-
hile the greatest minds in the country, in solemn assembly,
ad arranged a secret conference of city, state, and government
fficials, which Smurch was to attend for the purpose of being
astructed in the ethics and behavior of heroism.

On the day that the little mechanic was finally allowed to get
p and dress and, for the first time in two weeks, took a great
new of tobacco, he was permitted to receive the newspapermen
-this by way of testing him out. Smurch did not wait for ques-
ons. "Youse guys," he said—and the *Times* man winced—
youse guys can tell the cock-eyed world dat I put it over on
indbergh, see? Yeh—an' made an ass o' them two frogs." The
wo frogs" was a reference to a pair of gallant French fliers who,
 attempting a flight only halfway round the world, had, two
veeks before, unhappily been lost at sea. The *Times* man was
old enough, at this point, to sketch out for Smurch the accepted

formula for interviews in cases of this kind; he explained that there should be no arrogant statements belittling the achieve ments of other heroes, particularly heroes of foreign nation "Ah, the hell with that," said Smurch. "I did it, see? I did i an' I'm talkin' about it." And he did talk about it.

None of this extraordinary interview was, of course, printed On the contrary, the newspapers, already under the discipline direction of a secret directorate created for the occasion an composed of statesmen and editors, gave out to a panting an restless world that "Jacky," as he had been arbitrarily nick named, would consent to say only that he was very happy an that anyone could have done what he did. "My achievemen has been, I fear, slightly exaggerated," the *Times* man's articl had him protest, with a modest smile. These newspaper storie were kept from the hero, a restriction which did not serve t abate the rising malevolence of his temper. The situation wa indeed, extremely grave, for Pal Smurch was, as he kept insist ing, "rarin' to go." He could not much longer be kept from nation clamorous to lionize him. It was the most desperate crisi the United States of America had faced since the sinking of th *Lusitania*.

On the afternoon of the twenty-seventh of July, Smurch wa spirited away to a conference-room in which were gathere mayors, governors, government officials, behaviorist psycholo gists, and editors. He gave them each a limp, moist paw and brief unlovely grin. "Hah ya?" he said. When Smurch wa seated, the Mayor of New York arose and, with obvious pes simism, attempted to explain what he must say and how h must act when presented to the world, ending his talk with a high tribute to the hero's courage and integrity. The Mayo was followed by Governor Fanniman of New York, who, afte a touching declaration of faith, introduced Cameron Spottis wood, Second Secretary of the American Embassy in Paris, th gentleman selected to coach Smurch in the amenities of public ceremonies. Sitting in a chair, with a soiled yellow tie in his hand and his shirt open at the throat, unshaved, smoking a rolled cigarette, Jack Smurch listened with a leer on his lips. "I get ya, I get ya," he cut in, nastily. "Ya want me to ack like a softy, huh? Ya want me to ack like that —— —— baby-face Lindbergh, huh? Well, nuts to that, see?" Everyone took in his breath sharply; it was a sigh and a hiss. "Mr. Lindbergh," began a United States Senator, purple with rage, "and Mr. Byrd—" Smurch, who was paring his nails with a jackknife, cut in again. "Byrd!" he exclaimed. "Aw fa God's sake, *dat* big—" Somebody shut off his blasphemies with a sharp word. A newcomer had entered the room. Everyone stood up, except Smurch, who, still busy with his nails, did not even glance up. "Mr. Smurch," said someone, sternly, "the President of the United States!" It had been thought that the presence of the Chief Executive might have a chastening effect upon the young hero, and the former had been, thanks to the remarkable coöperation of the press, secretly brought to the obscure conference-room.

A great, painful silence fell. Smurch looked up, waved a hand at the President. "How ya comin'?" he asked, and began rolling a fresh cigarette. The silence deepened. Someone coughed in a strained way. "Geez, it's hot, ain't it?" said Smurch. He loosened two more shirt buttons, revealing a hairy chest and the tattooed word "Sadie" enclosed in a stencilled heart. The great and important men in the room, faced by the most serious crisis in recent American history, exchanged worried frowns. Nobody seemed to know how to proceed. "Come awn, come awn," said Smurch. "Let's get the hell out of here! When do I start cuttin' in on de parties, huh? And what's they goin' to be *in* it?" He rubbed a thumb and forefinger together meaningly. "Money!" exclaimed a state senator, shocked, pale. "Yeh, money," said Pal, flipping his cigarette out of a window.

) 211 (

"An' big money." He began rolling a fresh cigarette. "Big money," he repeated, frowning over the rice paper. He tilted back in his chair, and leered at each gentleman, separately, the leer of an animal that knows its power, the leer of a leopard loose in a bird-and-dog shop. "Aw fa God's sake, let's get some place where it's cooler," he said. "I been cooped up plenty for three weeks!"

Smurch stood up and walked over to an open window, where he stood staring down into the street, nine floors below. The faint shouting of newsboys floated up to him. He made out his name. "Hot dog!" he cried, grinning, ecstatic. He leaned out over the sill. "You tell 'em, babies!" he shouted down. "Hot diggity dog!" In the tense little knot of men standing behind him, a quick, mad impulse flared up. An unspoken word of appeal, of command, seemed to ring through the room. Yet it was deadly silent. Charles K. L. Brand, secretary to the Mayor of New York City, happened to be standing nearest Smurch; he looked inquiringly at the President of the United States. The President, pale, grim, nodded shortly. Brand, a tall, powerfully built man, once a tackle at Rutgers, stepped forward, seized the greatest man in the world by his left shoulder and the seat of his pants, and pushed him out the window.

"My God, he's fallen out the window!" cried a quick-witted editor.

"Get me out of here!" cried the President. Several men sprang to his side and he was hurriedly escorted out of a door toward a side-entrance of the building. The editor of the Associated Press took charge, being used to such things. Crisply he ordered certain men to leave, others to stay; quickly he outlined a story which all the papers were to agree on, sent two men to the street to handle that end of the tragedy, commanded a Senator to sob and two Congressmen to go to pieces nervously. In a word, he skillfully set the stage for the gigantic

task that was to follow, the task of breaking to a grief-stricken world the sad story of the untimely, accidental death of its most illustrious and spectacular figure.

The funeral was, as you know, the most elaborate, the finest, the solemnest, and the saddest ever held in the United States of America. The monument in Arlington Cemetery, with its clean white shaft of marble and the simple device of a tiny plane carved on its base, is a place for pilgrims, in deep reverence, to visit. The nations of the world paid lofty tributes to little Jacky Smurch, America's greatest hero. At a given hour there were two minutes of silence throughout the nation. Even the inhabitants of the small, bewildered town of Westfield, Iowa, observed this touching ceremony; agents of the Department of Justice saw to that. One of them was especially assigned to stand grimly in the doorway of a little shack restaurant on the edge of the tourists' camping ground just outside the town. There, under his stern scrutiny, Mrs. Emma Smurch bowed her head above two hamburger steaks sizzling on her grill—bowed her head and turned away, so that the Secret Service man could not see the twisted, strangely familiar, leer on her lips.

XXXV. One Is a Wanderer

THE walk up Fifth Avenue through the slush of the sidewalks and the dankness of the air had tired him. The dark was coming quickly down, the dark of a February Sunday evening, and that vaguely perturbed him. He didn't want to go "home," though, and get out of it. It would be gloomy and close in his hotel room, and his soiled shirts would be piled on the floor of the closet where he had been flinging them for weeks, where he had been flinging them for months, and his papers would be disarranged on the tops of the tables and on the desk, and his pipes would be lying around, the pipes he had smoked determinedly for a while only to give them up, as he always did, to go back to cigarettes. He turned into the street leading to his hotel, walking slowly, trying to decide what to do with the night. He had had too many nights alone. Once he had enjoyed being alone. Now it was hard to be alone. He couldn't read any more, or write, at night. Books he tossed aside after nervously flipping through them; the writing he tried to do turned into spirals and circles and squares and empty faces.

I'll just stop in, he thought, and see if there are any messages; I'll see if there have been any phone calls. He hadn't been back to the hotel, after all, for—let's see—for almost five hours; just wandering around. There might be some messages. I'll just stop in, he thought, and see; and maybe I'll have one brandy. I don't want to sit there in the lobby again and drink brandy; I don't want to do that.

He didn't go through the revolving doors of the hotel, though. He went on past the hotel and over to Broadway. A man asked him for some money. A shabbily dressed woman walked by, muttering. She had what he called the New York Mouth, a grim, set mouth, a strained, querulous mouth, a mouth that told of suffering and discontent. He looked in the window of a cane-and-umbrella shop and in the window of a cheap restaurant, a window holding artificial pie and cake, a cup of cold coffee, a plate of artificial vegetables. He got into the shoving and pushing and halting and slow flowing of Broadway. A big cop with a red face was striking his hands together and kidding with a couple of girls whom he had kept from crossing the street against a red light. A thin man in a thin overcoat watched them out of thin, emotionless eyes.

It was a momentary diversion to stand in front of the book counter in the drugstore at Forty-fifth Street and Broadway and look at the books, cheap editions of ancient favorites, movie editions of fairly recent best-sellers. He picked up some of the books and opened them and put them down again, but there was nothing he wanted to read. He walked over to the soda counter and sat down and asked for hot chocolate. It warmed him up a little and he thought about going to the movie at the Paramount; it was a movie with action and guns and airplanes, and Myrna Loy, the kind of movie that didn't bother you. He walked down to the theatre and stood there a minute, but he didn't buy a ticket. After all, he had been to one movie that day. He thought about going to the office. It would be quiet there, nobody would be there; maybe he could get some work done; maybe he could answer some of the letters he had been putting off for so long.

It was too gloomy, it was too lonely. He looked around the office for a while, sat down at his typewriter, tapped out the alphabet on a sheet of paper, took a paper-clip, straightened it, cleaned the "e" and the "o" on the typewriter, and put the cover over it. He never remembered to put the cover over the typewriter when he left in the evening. I never, as a matter of fact, remember anything, he thought. It is because I keep trying not to; I keep trying not to remember anything. It is an empty and cowardly thing, not to remember. It might lead you anywhere; no, it might stop you, it might stop you from getting anywhere. Out of remembrance comes everything; out of remembrance comes a great deal, anyway. You can't do anything if you don't let yourself remember things. He began to whistle a song because he found himself about to remember things, and he knew what things they would be, things that would bring a grimace to his mouth and to his eyes, disturbing fragments of old sentences, old scenes and gestures, hours, and rooms, and tones of voice, and the sound of a voice crying. All voices cry differently; there are no two voices in the whole world that cry alike; they're like footsteps and fingerprints and the faces of friends . . .

He became conscious of the song he was whistling. He got up from the chair in front of his covered typewriter, turned out the light, and walked out of the room to the elevator, and there he began to sing the last part of the song, waiting for the elevator. "Make my bed and light the light, for I'll be home late tonight, blackbird, bye bye." He walked over to his hotel through the slush and the damp gloom and sat down in a chair in the lobby, without taking off his overcoat. He didn't want to sit there long.

"Good evening, sir," said the waiter who looked after the guests in the lobby. "How are you?"

"I'm fine, thank you," he said. "I'm fine. I'll have a brandy, with water on the side."

He had several brandies. Nobody came into the lobby that he knew. People were gone to all kinds of places Sunday night. He hadn't looked at his letter box back of the clerk's desk when he came in, to see if there were any messages there. That was a kind of game he played, or something. He never looked for messages until after he had had a brandy. He'd look now after he had another brandy. He had another brandy and looked. "Nothing," said the clerk at the desk, looking too.

He went back to his chair in the lobby and began to think about calling up people. He thought of the Graysons. He saw the Graysons, not as they would be, sitting in their apartment, close together and warmly, but as he and Lydia had seen them in another place and another year. The four had shared a bright vacation once. He remembered various attitudes and angles and lights and colors of that vacation. There is something about four people, two couples, that like each other and get along; that have a swell time; that grow in intimacy and understanding. One's life is made up of twos, and of fours. The Graysons understood the nice little arrangements of living, the twos and fours. Two is company, four is a party, three is a crowd. One is a wanderer.

No, not the Graysons. Somebody would be there on Sunday night, some couple, some two; somebody he knew, somebody they had known. That is the way life is arranged. One arranges one's life—no, two arrange their life—in terms of twos, and fours, and sixes. Marriage does not make two people one, it makes two people two. It's sweeter that way, and simpler. All this, he thought, summoning the waiter, is probably very silly and sentimental. I must look out that I don't get to that state of tipsiness where all silly and lugubrious things seem brilliant divinations of mine, sound and original ideas and theories. What I must remember is that such things are sentimental and tiresome and grow out of not working enough and out of too much brandy. That's what I must remember. It is no good remembering that it takes four to make a party, two to make a house.

People living alone, after all, have made a great many things. Let's see, what have people living alone made? Not love, of course, but a great many other things: money, for example, and black marks on white paper. "Make this one a double brandy," he told the waiter. Let's see, who that I *know* has made something alone, who that I know *of* has made something alone? Robert Browning? No, not Robert Browning. Odd, that Robert Browning would be the first person he thought of. "And had you only heard me play one tune, or viewed me from a window, not so soon with you would such things fade as with the rest." He had written that line of Browning's in a book once for Lydia, or Lydia had written it in a book for him; or they had both written it in a book for each other. "Not so soon with you would such things fade as with the rest." Maybe he didn't have it exactly right; it was hard to remember now, after so long a time. It didn't matter. "Not so soon with you would such things fade as with the rest." The fact is that all things do fade; with twos, and with fours; all bright things, all attitudes and angles and lights and colors, all growing in intimacy and understanding.

I think maybe I'll call the Bradleys, he thought, getting up out of his chair. And don't, he said to himself, standing still a moment, don't tell me you're not cockeyed now, because you are cockeyed now, just as you said you wouldn't be when you got up this morning and had orange juice and coffee and determined to get some work done, a whole lot of work done; just as you said you wouldn't be but you knew you would be, all right. You knew you would be, all right.

The Bradleys, he thought, as he walked slowly around the lobby, avoiding the phone booths, glancing at the headlines of the papers on the newsstand, the Bradleys have that four-square thing, that two-square thing—that two-square thing, God damn them! Somebody described it once in a short story that he had read: an intimacy that you could feel, that you could almost take hold of, when you went into such a house, when you went into where such people were, a warming thing, a nice thing to be in, like being in warm sea water; a little embarrassing, too, yes, damned embarrassing, too. He would only take a damp blanket into that warmth. That's what I'd take into that warmth, he told himself, a damp blanket. They know it, too. Here comes old Kirk again with his damp blanket. It isn't because I'm so damned unhappy—I'm not so damned unhappy—it's because they're so damned happy, damn them. Why don't they know that? Why don't they do something about it? What right have they got to flaunt it at me, for God's sake? . . . Look here now, he told himself, you're getting too cockeyed now; you're getting into one of those states, you're getting into one of those states that Marianne keeps telling you about, one of those states when people don't like to have you around . . . Marianne, he thought. He went back to his chair, ordered another brandy, and thought about Marianne.

She doesn't know how I start my days, he thought, she only knows how I end them. She doesn't even know how I started my life. She only knows me when night gets me. If I could only be the person she wants me to be, why, then I would be fine, I would be the person she wants me to be. Like ordering a new dress from a shop, a new dress that nobody ever wore, a new dress that nobody's ever going to wear but you. I wouldn't get mad suddenly, about nothing. I wouldn't walk out of places suddenly, about nothing. I wouldn't snarl at nice people. About what she says is nothing. I wouldn't be "unbearable." Her word, "unbearable." A female word, female as a cat. Well, she's right, to. I am unbearable. "George," he said to the waiter, "I am unbearable, did you know that?" "No, sir, I did not, sir," said the waiter. "I would not call you unbearable, Mr. Kirk." "Well, you don't know, George," he said. "It just happens that I am unbearable. It just happened that way. It's a long story." "Yes, sir," said the waiter.

I could call up the Mortons, he thought. They'll have twos and fours there, too, but they're not so damned happy that they're unbearable. The Mortons are all right. Now look, the Mortons had said to him, if you and Marianne would only stop fighting and arguing and forever analyzing yourselves and forever analyzing everything, you'd be fine. You'd be fine if you got married and just shut up, just shut up and got married. That would be fine. Yes, sir, that would be fine. Everything would work out all right. You just shut up and get married, you just get married and shut up. Everybody knows that. It is practically the simplest thing in the world. . . . Well, it would be, too, if you were twenty-five maybe; it would be if you were twenty-five, and not forty.

"George," he said, when the waiter walked over for his empty glass, "I will be forty-one next November." "But that's not old, sir, and that's a long way off," said George. "No, it isn't," he said. "It's almost here. So is forty-two and forty-three and fifty, and here I am trying to be—do you know what I'm trying to be, George? I'm trying to be happy." "We all want to be happy, sir," said George. "I would like to see you happy, sir." "Oh, you will," he said. "You will, George. There's a simple trick to it. You just shut up and get married. But you see, George, I am an analyzer. I am also a rememberer. I have a pocketful of old used years. You put all those things together and they sit in a lobby getting silly and old." "I'm very sorry, sir," said George.

) 221 (

"And I'll have one more drink, George," he called after the waiter.

He had one more drink. When he looked up at the clock in the lobby it was only 9:30. He went up to his room and, feeling sleepy, he lay down on his bed without turning out the overhead light. When he woke up it was 12:30 by his wristwatch. He got up and washed his face and brushed his teeth and put on a clean shirt and another suit and went back down into the lobby, without looking at the disarranged papers on the table and on the desk. He went into the dining-room and had some soup and a lamb chop and a glass of milk. There was nobody there he knew. He began to realize that he had to see somebody he knew. He paid his check and went out and got into a cab and gave the driver an address on Fifty-third Street.

There were several people in Dick and Joe's that he knew. There were Dick and Joe, for two—or, rather, for one, because he always thought of them as one; he could never tell them apart. There were Bill Vardon and Mary Wells. Bill Vardon and Mary Wells were a little drunk and gay. He didn't know them very well, but he could sit down with them. . . .

It was after three o'clock when he left the place and got into a cab. "How are you tonight, Mr. Kirk?" asked the driver. The driver's name was Willie. "I'm fine tonight, Willie," he said. "You want to go on somewheres else?" asked Willie. "Not tonight, Willie," he said. "I'm going home." "Well," said Willie, "I guess you're right there, Mr. Kirk. I guess you're right about that. These places is all right for what they are—you know what I mean—it's O.K. to kick around in 'em for a while and maybe have a few drinks with your friends, but when you come right down to it, home is the best place there is. Now you take me, I'm hackin' for ten years, mostly up around here —because why? Because all these places know me; you know that, Mr. Kirk. I can get into 'em you might say the same way

ou do, Mr. Kirk—I have me a couple drinks in Dick and
oe's maybe or in Tony's or anywheres else I want to go into—
ell, I've had drinks in 'em with you, Mr. Kirk—like on
hristmas night, remember? But I got a home over in Brook-
n and a wife and a couple kids and, boy, I'm tellin' you that's
e best place, you know what I mean?"

"You're right, Willie," he said. "You're absolutely right,
ere."

"You're darn tootin' I am," said Willie. "These joints is all
ght when a man wants a couple drinks or maybe even get a
ttle tight with his friends, that's O.K. with me——"

"Getting tight with friends is O.K. with me, too," he said to
Willie.

"But when a man gets fed up on that kind of stuff, a man
ants to go home. Am I right, Mr. Kirk?"

"You're absolutely right, Willie," he said. "A man wants to
o home."

"Well, here we are, Mr. Kirk. Home it is."

He got out of the cab and gave the driver a dollar and told
im to keep the change and went into the lobby of the hotel.
he night clerk gave him his key and then put two fingers
nto the recesses of the letter box. "Nothing," said the night
lerk.

When he got to his room, he lay down on the bed a while
nd smoked a cigarette. He found himself feeling drowsy and
e got up. He began to take his clothes off, feeling drowsily
ontented, mistily contented. He began to sing, not loudly,
ecause the man in 711 would complain. The man in 711 was a
ray-haired man, living alone . . . an analyzer . . . a remem-
erer . . .

"Make my bed and light the light, for I'll be home late to-
ight . . ."

I WAITED till the large woman with the awful hat took up he
sack of groceries and went out, peering at the tomatoes an
lettuce on her way. The clerk asked me what mine was.

"Have you got a box," I asked, "a large box? I want a box t
hide in."

"You want a box?" he asked.

"I want a box to hide in," I said.

"Whatta you mean?" he said. "You mean a big box?"

I said I meant a big box, big enough to hold me.

"I haven't got any boxes," he said. "Only cartons that can
come in."

I tried several other groceries and none of them had a bo
big enough for me to hide in. There was nothing for it but t
face life out. I didn't feel strong, and I'd had this overpowerin;
desire to hide in a box for a long time.

"Whatta you mean you want to hide in this box?" on
grocer asked me.

"It's a form of escape," I told him, "hiding in a box. It circumscribes your worries and the range of your anguish. You don't see people, either."

"How in the hell do you eat when you're in this box?" asked the grocer. "How in the hell do you get anything to eat?" I said I had never been in a box and didn't know, but that that would take care of itself.

"Well," he said, finally, "I haven't got any boxes, only some pasteboard cartons that cans come in."

It was the same every place. I gave up when it got dark and the groceries closed, and hid in my room again. I turned out the light and lay on the bed. You feel better when it gets dark. I could have hid in a closet, I suppose, but people are always opening doors. Somebody would find you in a closet. They would be startled and you'd have to tell them why you were in the closet. Nobody pays any attention to a big box lying on the floor. You could stay in it for days and nobody'd think to look in it, not even the cleaning-woman.

My cleaning-woman came the next morning and woke me up. I was still feeling bad. I asked her if she knew where I could get a large box.

"How big a box you want?" she asked.

"I want a box big enough for me to get inside of," I said. She looked at me with big, dim eyes. There's something wrong with her glands. She's awful but she has a big heart, which makes it worse. She's unbearable, her husband is sick and her children are sick and she is sick too. I got to thinking how pleasant it would be if I were in a box now, and didn't have to see her. I would be in a box right there in the room and she wouldn't know. I wondered if you have a desire to bark or laugh when someone who doesn't know walks by the box you are in. Maybe she would have a spell with her heart, if I did that, and would die right there. The officers and the elevatorman and Mr.

Gramadge would find us. "Funny doggone thing happened a the building last night," the doorman would say to his wife "I let in this woman to clean up 10-F and she never come out see? She's never there more'n an hour, but she never come out see? So when it got to be time for me to go off duty, why says to Crennick, who was on the elevator, I says what the hel you suppose has happened to that woman cleans 10-F? H says he didn't know; he says he never seen her after he took her up. So I spoke to Mr. Gramadge about it. 'I'm sorry to bother you, Mr. Gramadge,' I says, 'but there's something funny about that woman cleans 10-F.' So I told him. So he said we better have a look and we all three goes up and knocks on the door and rings the bell, see, and nobody answers so he said we'd have to walk in so Crennick opened the door and we walked in and here was this woman cleans the apartment dead as a herring on the floor and the gentleman that lives there was in a box." . . .

The cleaning-woman kept looking at me. It was hard to realize she wasn't dead. "It's a form of escape," I murmured "What say?" she asked, dully.

"You don't know of any large packing boxes, do you?" I asked.

"No, I don't," she said.

I haven't found one yet, but I still have this overpowering urge to hide in a box. Maybe it will go away, maybe I'll be all right. Maybe it will get worse. It's hard to say.